HISTORY OF
THE ANCIENT AND MEDIEVAL WORLD

SECOND EDITION

VOLUME 9

WESTERN ASIA, NORTHERN EUROPE,
AND AFRICA IN THE MIDDLE AGES

Marshall Cavendish
Reference
New York

Marshall Cavendish
99 White Plains Road
Tarrytown, New York 10591

www.marshallcavendish.us

Library of Congress Cataloging-in-Publication Data

History of the ancient and medieval world / [edited by Henk Dijkstra]. --
2nd ed.
    v. cm.
 Includes bibliographical references and index.
 Contents: v. 1. The first civilizations -- v. 2. Western Asia and the
Mediterranean -- v. 3. Ancient Greece -- v. 4. The Roman Empire -- v. 5. The
changing shape of Europe -- v. 6. The early Middle Ages in western Asia and
Europe -- v. 7. Southern and eastern Asia -- v. 8. Europe in the Middle Ages
-- v. 9. Western Asia, northern Europe, and Africa in the Middle Ages -- v.
10. The passing of the medieval world -- v. 11. Index.
 ISBN 978-0-7614-7789-1 (set) -- ISBN 978-0-7614-7791-4 (v. 1) -- ISBN
978-0-7614-7792-1 (v. 2) -- ISBN 978-0-7614-7793-8 (v. 3) -- ISBN
978-0-7614-7794-5 (v. 4) -- ISBN 978-0-7614-7795-2 (v. 5) -- ISBN
978-0-7614-7796-9 (v. 6) -- ISBN 978-0-7614-7797-6 (v. 7) -- ISBN
978-0-7614-7798-3 (v. 8) -- ISBN 978-0-7614-7799-0 (v. 9) -- ISBN
978-0-7614-7800-3 (v. 10) -- ISBN 978-0-7614-7801-0 (v. 11)
1. History, Ancient. 2. Middle Ages. 3. Civilization, Medieval. I.
Dijkstra, Henk.
 D117.H57 2009
 940.1--dc22

                          2008060052

Printed in Malaysia

12 11 10 09 08 7 6 5 4 3 2 1

General Editor: Henk Dijkstra

Marshall Cavendish
Project Editor: Brian Kinsey
Publisher: Paul Bernabeo
Production Manager: Michael Esposito

Brown Reference Group
Project Editor: Chris King
Text Editors: Shona Grimbly, Charles Phillips
Designer: Lynne Lennon
Cartographers: Joan Curtis, Darren Awuah
Picture Researcher: Laila Torsun
Indexer: Christine Michaud
Managing Editor: Tim Cooke

PICTURE CREDITS

SET CONTENTS

VOLUME CONTENTS

THE EARLY BYZANTINE EMPIRE

After the western part of the Roman Empire succumbed to barbarian invasions in the fifth century CE, the eastern part (now known as the Byzantine Empire) flourished independently. It was ruled from Constantinople, formerly known as Byzantium.

The success and the very nature of the Byzantine Empire—as the eastern part of the old Roman Empire became known—were attributable partly to chance and a combination of circumstances. Mainly, however, the new power center thrived as a result of three deliberate and astute political moves: the recognition of Christianity, the reform of the currency, and the establishment of Constantinople as its capital.

The early Byzantine rulers were also Roman emperors. Diocletian (ruled 284–305 CE) and Constantine I (sole emperor 324–337 CE) were both soldiers who imposed military discipline on a previously anarchic body politic; they even imposed their sense of order on religious affairs.

Constantine was particularly important, because it was during his reign that the imperial Roman leadership system of co-emperors was finally acknowledged as unworkable and was replaced with a formal transfer of power within a single ruling family, often but not always from father to son. By the end of the fourth century CE, the dynastic principle was well established. Theodosius I was the last emperor to rule the unified Roman Empire. When he died in 395 CE, he divided his land between his sons, bequeathing the west to Honorius and the east to Arcadius.

Another of Constantine's great achievements was the regionalization of power. The success of local devolution and the separation of military authority from civilian government demonstrated that outlying provinces could be allowed a certain amount of political freedom without necessarily endangering the empire as a cohesive whole.

Constantine was a Christian convert who raised the status of his new faith to that of a "permitted religion." In the short term, it was a response to a popular trend; in the longer term, it helped to establish the religion permanently in southeastern Europe. Constantine also brought in a new currency, the gold solidus, which replaced the debased old denarius and remained the standard for centuries. Constantine transferred the capital of the empire from Rome to Byzantium, which he renamed Constantinople after himself in 330 CE.

Migration and prosperity

In the second half of the fourth century CE, the Huns (a nomadic people who originated to the east of the Volga River) began attacking the Ostrogoths and the Visigoths (early Germanic peoples) and

This mosaic, depicting Mary and Jesus, is one of the oldest treasures in the Hagia Sophia, the main church built in Constantinople.

THE EARLY BYZANTINE EMPIRE

KEY

Byzantine Empire in 628 CE

✗ Major battle

drove them west and south across the Danube River. Some of them sought refuge in the rapidly disintegrating Roman Empire, but they were exploited there by their new hosts. In 378 CE, they rose and scored an important victory against the Romans at the Battle of Adrianople (modern Edirne, in European Turkey).

Later, the imperial rulers accepted the need to coexist with the Goths. Theodosius I (ruled 379–395 CE) granted the Goths lands and gave them the status of *foederati* (allies). Having gained a measure of acceptance, the Goths later fought on the side of the Romans in several military campaigns.

In another significant development, Christianity became more than just an option. After 391 CE, the religion started to become a requirement. Tolerance of other faiths diminished; priests and politicians first defined heresy and then looked for ways to eradicate it. A new era of persecution was at hand.

Meanwhile, Constantinople became one of the world's most prosperous cities. Its wealth, based primarily on trade throughout the region, was boosted by a sudden influx of gold. The exact origin of the precious metal is unknown, but it may have come from newly discovered deposits in outlying regions or else from the looting of pagan temples.

Constantinople's wealth was a magnet for people from all over eastern Europe and the Mediterranean who flocked to the city in search of work and security; the fortress had earned a reputation for impregnability, and indeed, it remained unbreached until the Fourth Crusade in 1204 CE. Although there are no exact population figures, it is believed that, by the fifth century CE, Constantinople had at least 200,000 inhabitants and may have had as many as 500,000, making it by far the most populous city in the world at the time. Having previously welcomed growth, the emperors became alarmed at the rate of increase and sought to restrict the number of residents by taxation and by imposing stricter requirements for citizenship.

The Huns

During the fifth century CE, the greatest threat to the Byzantine Empire came from the northeast, where the forces of Attila the Hun (ruled 434–453 CE) massed against it in the Balkans, in the Caucasus, and in parts of what is now Russia. Attila's troops captured and destroyed Singidunum (modern Belgrade, Serbia) in 441 CE and the cities of Nis and Sofia in 443 CE. Advancing southward, the Huns then set their sights on Constantinople, but having occupied the lands to the north and south of the city, Attila decided that his army—composed principally of archers—would be unable to storm it. The emperor Theodosius II (ruled 408–450 CE) negotiated a truce with the

This Roman fresco, produced in 1246 CE, depicts Sylvester I, the pope who converted the emperor Constantine to Christianity.

This photograph shows modern Istanbul, the name adopted in 1930 CE by the city formerly known as Constantinople.

Huns and agreed to pay an annual tribute of 2,100 pounds of gold. The ensuing peace was uneasy, but Byzantine traders maximized the commercial opportunities; it appears that Constantinople benefited greatly from its subsequent trade with the Huns.

Full independence

From 474 to 491 CE, the Byzantine Empire was ruled by Zeno, an Isaurian (from Anatolia, modern Turkey). The Byzantines had welcomed the Isaurian people to help them in their struggle against northern invaders, but once that danger had passed, they strove to rid themselves of Turkish influence. When Zeno died, his widow, Ariadne, married Anastasius, who succeeded to the imperial throne. The Isaurians tried to resist their loss of power, but their period of dominance was over, at least for the time

being. Meanwhile, the Roman Empire finally disintegrated and the Byzantine Empire became an independent power.

Orthodoxy and heresy

Although Christianity was now firmly established as the Byzantine religion, it was divided by internal controversies. The main point of contention was the teaching of Arius (c. 250–336 CE), a priest from Alexandria who argued that God and Christ were essentially different because God the Father had existed from the start of eternity, while God the Son was a child in time. Arius's theory had been rejected by the Christian church at the Council of Nicaea in 325 CE, but the idea—subsequently known as the Arian heresy—persisted in the fourth century CE and was definitively condemned only in 381 CE with promulgation at the Council of Aquileia of the doctrine that Father and Son were of one substance and thus coexistent.

However, the resolution of the Arian problem created a new theological difficulty as Christians argued about how to reconcile the human and divine elements of their deity. In the fifth century CE, two schools of thought emerged. One school, based in Alexandria, took the view that God the Father and God the Son were indistinguishable. That theory was known as Monophysitism. The other theory, known as Dyophysitism and based in Antioch, contended that both natures coexisted separately in Christ.

The argument fueled a struggle for power between the three main branches of the Christian church. In 428 CE, Nestorius, patriarch (archbishop) of Constantinople, ruled in favor of Dyophysitism. In Rome, Pope Leo I (ruled 440–461 CE) took the same view. Only Alexandria adopted Monophysitism as the true faith, and being in a minority, the Egyptian branch of Christianity gradually became sidelined.

Justinian

When the last emperor in Rome, Romulus Augustulus, was deposed by the German warrior Odoacer in 476 CE, the eastern part of the old empire comprised the Balkan Peninsula, much of southwestern Asia, Palestine, Egypt, and northeastern Africa. When the emperor Justinian (ruled 527–565 CE) came to the throne in Constantinople, he extended Byzantine power even farther. The Byzantine armies retained the military cohesion and discipline that had been features of the armies of the Roman Empire, and Justinian employed generals of genius such as Belisarius. Byzantine forces took northern Africa, Italy, part of Spain, and the Mediterranean islands of Sicily and Sardinia. At its peak, around 550 CE, Justinian's empire almost encircled the Mediterranean.

Justinian's achievements as a conqueror were matched by his prowess as a legislator. He sought to eradicate corruption and provide justice for all his subjects, objectives that could not be

This 12th-century-CE French enamel plaque depicts the Byzantine emperor Heraclius receiving a visitation from the Old Testament prophet Ezekiel.

This mosaic, depicting an eagle and a snake, was installed on one of the floors of the imperial palace in Constantinople during the reign of the emperor Justinian (ruled 527–565 CE).

achieved without a radical reorganization of the legal system. He produced a new constitution in 529 CE and a classic handbook for law students, the *Institutiones* (Institutes), in 534 CE. In 535 CE, he banned the sale of provincial governorships, a previously frequent practice.

While Justinian was preoccupied with those and other projects, he delegated domestic administration to two outstanding deputies, John of Cappadocia and Peter Barsymes. Their primary task—to raise sufficient revenue to maintain imperial territories—was not straightforward, because many of the frontier provinces were too poor to sustain themselves. The two ministers solved the problem by taxing imports, particularly spices, perfumes, and silk.

Internal revolt

The taxation and the emperor's war on corruption were deeply unpopular with the inhabitants of Constantinople. In 532 CE, the city's two main political factions—the Blues and the Greens—united in an uprising known as the Nika Revolt, from the Greek word for "victory." The rebels ran riot, setting fire to several public buildings and part of the imperial palace. When no one confronted them, they called for Justinian to be replaced by Hypatius, the nephew of the late emperor Anastasius (ruled 491–518 CE). For a time, it looked as if the rebels might prevail, but then troops led by Belisarius intervened and restored order by massacring the insurgents. Hypatius was later put to death.

Foreign threats

Justinian laid the foundation of the Byzantine Empire, but he did not complete its construction. He left enormous challenges for his successors. The key strategic problems were that the frontiers of the Byzantine Empire in Italy and the Balkans were still periodically threatened by barbarian invaders while the eastern borders were confronted with a succession of threats, first from the Persian Sassanid Empire, then from Arabs who were spreading Islam by the sword, and finally from central Asian Turkic peoples who themselves created powerful empires.

By the end of the sixth century CE, the Byzantine Empire had surrendered most of its territory in northern Italy to the Lombards. The Balkans were ravaged, first by Avar raiders from the Caucasus and later by Slavic tribes who moved in to claim great swathes of undefended Byzantine territory.

The assassination of the emperor Maurice (ruled 582–602 CE) ushered in a period of civil strife in the Byzantine Empire. In 610 CE, a soldier named Heraclius seized the throne from Maurice's successor, the incompetent and despotic Phocas. Sensing a power vacuum, the Avars and Persians promptly invaded the Byzantine Empire. In 622 CE, Heraclius counterattacked, despatching the Avars back to central Europe and driving the Persians from Anatolia, Egypt, and Syria. In 628 CE, Heraclius invaded Persia itself.

The next major challenge to the Byzantine Empire came from the Arab armies that swarmed westward from the Arabian Peninsula. The Arabs enjoyed

This Byzantine solidus (gold coin) was minted in the seventh century CE.

great early success, defeating Persian forces, conquering the Sassanid Empire, and taking over many of the eastern provinces of the Byzantine Empire, including Syria and Egypt. They attacked Constantinople itself in the 670s CE, but in the face of ferocious opposition, they were unable to surmount the city walls.

Leo III

In the early eighth century CE, the Byzantine Empire was attacked simultaneously on three fronts by the Slavs, the Bulgars, and the Arabs. From 717 to 718 CE, Constantinople itself was besieged. The emperor Theodosius III was overthrown in 717 CE by his leading general, who took the throne as Leo III. Leo and his family became known as the Isaurian dynasty, but unlike Zeno, they came from Syria rather than Anatolia. Having fought off the Arabs on land and at sea, Leo established a state that remained stable for the following 300 years. The frontiers of the eighth-century-CE Byzantine Empire were secured by an army of up to 150,000 men, most of whom served in cataphracts (units of armored archers on horseback) that were deployed along the eastern edges of Anatolia and Thrace (Asia Minor and northern Greece).

Having secured the frontiers of his empire, Leo set about modernizing its legal system. In 726 CE, he issued a new code, the *Ecloga*, which revised the precepts established in the sixth century CE by the emperor Justinian. The *Ecloga* paid particular attention to property rights and the regulation of marriage along

Christian lines. It also reduced the maximum penalty for several offenses from death to amputation and mutilation. In order to reduce corruption, Leo made judges salaried employees of the state rather than volunteers, so they would be less susceptible to bribery.

Iconoclasm

When Leo turned his attention to religion, he ordered the forced baptism of all Byzantine Jews and various Christian sects that he decreed heretical. Then, in 730 CE, the emperor introduced iconoclasm, the measure for which he is principally remembered.

At the time, many Christians worshipped images of God and holy relics (sacred objects, such as pieces of wood that were believed to come from the cross on which Jesus was crucified). They were known as iconodules. Other Christians, however, believed that such practices were sacrilegious. They were known as iconoclasts, from the Greek for "destroyers of images."

For many years, the two forms of worship coexisted, but mutual tolerance ended abruptly after Leo made iconoclasm imperial policy. Leo's proclamation gave the iconoclasts authority to raid churches and remove and destroy all the sacred images they found there. The campaign began in earnest with the demolition of the great gold icon of Christ beside the Bronze Gate that led to the royal palace in Constantinople. The act caused outrage among Leo's subjects. The commander of the demolition squad was attacked and killed by a group of women. Undeterred, Leo persevered with his campaign. When Germanus I, the patriarch of Constantinople, condemned the attacks, Leo had him removed from office and replaced by one of his own sympathizers, Anastasius. For minor opponents of iconoclasm, the penalties were harsher. Clerics who tried to resist the emperor's will were beaten and thrown in jail.

In 734 CE, Leo issued a decree that not only icons but all representations of the human figure in religious art should be destroyed and that any failure to do so would be harshly punished. At first, the decree created an uproar, but eventually, the churchmen of the empire agreed that Leo's controversial decision should be upheld. All icons were smashed, and all statues were removed from their plinths.

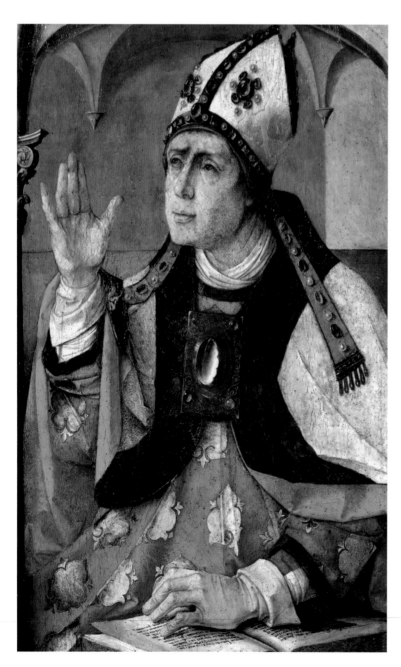

The controversy over the worship of icons then abated, but it resurfaced periodically thereafter and remained an important issue in Byzantine society until 847 CE.

Leo encountered further opposition from Rome, where popes Gregory II (ruled 715–731 CE) and Gregory III (ruled 731–741 CE) warned the emperor against any attempt to implement iconoclasm in Byzantine territories in southern Italy. Leo retaliated by cutting financial aid to the papacy and decreeing that churches in Sicily and Calabria should break with Rome and come under the jurisdiction of the eastern patriarch. The vehemence of Leo's response alarmed the papacy, which was forced to turn to the Frankish rulers for support. As a result, there was a westward shift in the balance of power that gradually weakened Byzantine influence on the Italian Peninsula. The enmities created by the iconoclasm struggle disrupted the Byzantine Empire for more than a hundred years.

Roman influence wanes

During the early Middle Ages, the Byzantine Empire became less Roman and more Greek, even though, as late as the seventh century CE, the emperors still addressed their subjects as *Romaioi* (Romans). Foreigners called Byzantine citizens *Graeci* (Greeks), because Greek was the language used for all the empire's administrative, scientific, and educational purposes. In addition to Greek, Coptic (the language of ancient Egypt), Syriac, and Armenian were among a host of tongues that were widely spoken in the Byzantine Empire. However, Latin was no longer used, and the abandonment of the language of Rome was an eloquent symbol of the division of the old empire.

By the reign of Leo III, the emperor himself was no longer titled *caesar* or *imperator* (emperor). Instead, he was called

This fifth-century-CE Byzantine ivory carving depicts Adam in paradise.

basileus, the Greek word for king or emperor. The *basileus* was the source of all secular law and governmental authority. He also played a vital part in religious matters. He was expected to lend imperial authority to church doctrine and had the final say in selecting the patriarch of Constantinople, as well as making all political and military appointments.

See also:

THE MIDDLE AND LATE BYZANTINE EMPIRE

After around 150 years of territorial expansion, the Byzantine Empire peaked in the 11th century CE. Its decline began after the Battle of Manzikert in 1071 CE. By the middle of the 15th century CE, it had completely disintegrated.

The emperor Leo III, who had rescued the Byzantine Empire during a period of great crisis (717–718 CE), left a legacy of discord by banning religious images (icons), a policy known as iconoclasm. Over the following three centuries, the conflicts generated by the dispute over iconoclasm were gradually resolved and the Byzantine Empire enjoyed periods of great success, especially in the early 11th century CE. However, a military defeat by Turkish forces in 1071 CE caused serious difficulties. The empire struggled to recover, especially when crusaders from western Europe sacked Constantinople in 1204 CE.

Under Leo's successors, iconoclasm remained the official policy, but after the reign of his son, Constantine V (ruled 741–775 CE), it was less rigorously pursued. Leo's grandson, Leo IV (ruled 775–780 CE), married into an aristocratic Athenian family. His wife, Irene, was ambitious, scheming, and cruel. She was an iconodule (one who believes that icons are a means of achieving a religious experience). Despite the official edicts against the veneration of images, her husband raised no objection to her method of worship.

The merciless Irene

In the beginning, Irene stayed in the background. Then, in 780 CE, Leo was incapacitated by a virulent fever. When he died in September of that year, leaving a 10-year-old son, Irene lost no time in securing the regency for herself. Although her child was nominally the emperor Constantine VI, Irene was the power behind the throne for the next 11 years.

With her newly acquired authority, Irene sought to promote the veneration of icons. When the patriarch (bishop) of Constantinople resigned in 784 CE, Irene appointed her secretary, Tarasius, in his place. Following Irene's iconodule policy, Tarasius decided that relations with Rome must be restored. Accordingly, western churchmen were invited to an ecumenical council at Nicaea (modern Iznik, Turkey) in 787 CE for the purpose of condemning iconoclasm. The council duly did so, with the proviso that icons were to be venerated rather than worshipped.

The regent's interference in religious affairs aroused great ill-feeling among the Byzantine people. Young Constantine VI became a rallying point for their discontent. When Irene uncovered a conspiracy against her, she put Constantine in prison and decreed that every soldier in the army should swear a personal oath of allegiance

This ceremonial chalice was crafted for the coronation of the Byzantine emperor Romanus II in 959 CE.

This solidus (gold coin) bears the effigy of Irene, the first woman to rule the Byzantine Empire.

palace. His mother then ordered that his eyes should be gouged out. The emperor died shortly afterward from his injuries.

Irene's subsequent conduct did nothing to improve her reputation as a cruel despot. Rather than following tradition and choosing a husband to rule, she had herself crowned empress. She made a bid for popularity by lowering taxes, but that merely crippled the empire's finances.

Charlemagne

On Christmas Day of 800 CE, Pope Leo III crowned the king of the Franks, Charlemagne, as Holy Roman emperor. There had been no emperor in the west for more than 400 years. The coronation had enormous symbolic significance; by performing it, the pope was claiming supremacy over the emperor. Constantinople was rocked by the news, feeling that the pope had acted with unparalleled arrogance.

Soon, another event caused even greater consternation. Charlemagne proposed marriage to Irene, and the empress expressed her readiness to accept. The union made sound political sense. For Charlemagne, it was an opportunity to unite the western and eastern empires under his own rule. For Irene, it was a chance to save her empire from bankruptcy. The wedding never took place, however. Irene lost her throne in 802 CE in a bloodless palace revolution led by Nicephorus, the minister of finance. She was exiled to the island of Lesbos and died in the following year. Irene was the last ruler of the Isaurian dynasty.

Three emperors in one decade

The new emperor, Nicephorus I, did his best to repair the economic and political

to her. However, the Armeniakoi, an Armenian regiment of great military and political importance, mutinied. Constantine was proclaimed sole ruler. Irene was held under guard in her palace, and Constantine was crowned emperor.

In spite of his initial popularity, Constantine soon alienated most of his supporters. His foreign policy was a disaster. He concluded a humiliating peace treaty with invading Arabs and fled the battlefield during a confrontation with the Bulgars. When Constantine divorced his first wife and married another woman, even the iconodules lost patience with him. Irene was recalled to court, and behind the scenes, she reassembled her supporters and prepared to form a new government.

One day, when Constantine was out riding, he was taken prisoner by a party of soldiers and brought back to the damage caused by his predecessor. He established diplomatic relations with Charlemagne, put the imperial finances in order, and organized military campaigns against the pagan Bulgars who were invading from the north. For a time, the campaigns were successful. However, in July of 811 CE, Nicephorus, his army, and his son Stauracius were ambushed by Bulgars. Nicephorus was killed, along with many of his soldiers; Stauracius was severely injured and left with a broken back.

For two months, Stauracius tried to govern from his sickbed, but when it became clear that the Byzantine Empire could not be ruled effectively by an invalid, he was persuaded to abdicate in favor of his brother-in-law Michael.

As emperor, Michael turned out to be weak-willed and profligate with money. Nevertheless, it was during his short reign that the eastern and western emperors signed a treaty, known as the Pax Nicephori, that upheld both rulers' rights to imperial status. Each emperor was free to pursue his own policies while respecting those of the other.

Meanwhile, the Bulgars, led by Khan Krum, were posing a renewed threat. At the Battle of Versinicia in June of 813 CE, Michael confronted the invaders with a force of mainly Macedonian and Anatolian troops. The Anatolians deserted, leaving the Macedonian contingent to be slaughtered. Michael escaped to Constantinople, where he abdicated. The throne was taken by an Armenian commander named Leo, who had been in charge of the Anatolians. Michael was banished to a monastery, where he died in 841 CE.

Armenians on the throne

Leo V (ruled 813–820 CE) was a moderate iconoclast. He worked to restore the economy and the military organization of the Byzantine Empire. His reign was ended by a conspiracy. A close assistant to the emperor was arrested, but with the help of his guard, the prisoner managed to get word to his fellow plotters, and on the following morning, disguised as monks, they infiltrated the palace chapel and assassinated Leo during a service. With chains still around his feet, Michael II was crowned emperor.

The new ruler's first great challenge was a rebellion in Anatolia (part of modern Turkey) led by Thomas the Slav, who had once been a friend and fellow officer of the new *basileus* (emperor) and his predecessor. Although elderly, Thomas

This 12th-century-CE Byzantine reliquary (box for holy objects) contains a small piece of wood that is said to be a fragment of the cross on which Jesus Christ was crucified.

This 12th-century-CE manuscript illumination depicts the coronation of the Byzantine emperor Michael I in 811 CE.

was a charismatic figure who won the support of disgruntled members of Byzantine society. He recruited a huge army of dissatisfied farmers and adventurers and, with Muslim support, laid siege to the capital, Constantinople. The people of Constantinople resisted, and eventually, the Bulgars, who had made a peace treaty with the Byzantines, offered to help. Early in 823 CE, a Bulgarian horde attacked the besieging army and cut it to pieces. Thomas escaped, but later in the year, he was captured, brought before the emperor, and sentenced to have his hands and feet cut off before being impaled on a stake.

During the ninth century CE, the Byzantine Empire engaged in a series of wars against the Muslim caliphate in Baghdad and the Bulgars in the Balkans,

in Italy, and at sea. The power of the Muslim caliphate was waning, however, and the Byzantine armies remained strong. Under Michael's son, Theophilus (ruled 829–842 CE), Constantinople prospered as never before.

Theophilus embarked on an extravagant building program and decorated his own palace in lavish Arab style. Yet, despite his admiration for all things Islamic, Theophilus was forced to fight constant border wars against the caliph. Although the emperor was himself an iconoclast, he did not inquire too closely into what his subjects did in their own homes. Indeed, his own wife, Theodora, took the view that artistic representation of the sacred was acceptable.

On the death of Theophilus, Theodora took over the government on behalf of their three-year-old son, Michael. As empress, one of Theodora's first concerns was to get rid of iconoclasm. In 843 CE, she convened the Council of Orthodoxy, which declared that the veneration of icons was now legitimate and branded leading iconoclasts, living and dead, as heretics. (Theodora stipulated, however, that her late husband should not be one of those denounced.) That decision led to the end of iconoclasm in 847 CE.

On reaching adulthood, Theodora's son became the emperor Michael III. He was weak and indecisive and preferred a life of leisure to the responsibilities of office. For a time, Michael delegated his duties to his uncle, Bardas, while he himself went drinking with a friend named Basil, an ambitious Armenian peasant.

Basil made himself indispensable to Michael and rose to become lord chamberlain. In 866 CE, Basil arranged to have Bardas assassinated. Almost immediately afterward, Michael appointed Basil as co-emperor.

Michael then declined into alcohol dependency and became an embarrassment to his co-emperor. On the night of September 27, 867 CE, Basil and a gang of accomplices entered the imperial bedchamber and hacked Michael to death while he slept.

The Macedonian dynasty

As sole emperor, Basil I founded the Macedonian dynasty, which ruled for more than 200 years. His first contact with the man who would make him co-

This Byzantine armband from the ninth century CE is made from sheets of gold and decorated with enamel paint.

1173

emperor had been through his work as a stable hand in the imperial stables. However, although Basil was illiterate and uneducated, he proved to be an outstandingly competent emperor.

During his reign (867–886 CE), Basil strengthened his armed forces and won important victories over Muslim forces, particularly in southern Italy. He reformed the administration of government and began an overhaul of the legal system—eventually completed by his son, Leo VI (ruled 886–912 CE).

Leo's son, Constantine VII, was only eight years old when he inherited the throne. For a while, his mother, the empress Zoe, acted as regent, but her unpopular policies provoked an uprising. In 920 CE, a Byzantine admiral, Romanus Lecapenus, seized power and was crowned co-emperor with Constantine. Having consolidated his position by forcing a marriage between his daughter and Constantine, Romanus I ruled for almost a quarter of a century (920–944 CE) before he retired to a monastery, leaving Constantine to rule alone.

Constantine VII had a gentle, retiring nature and devoted much of his life to literary pursuits. While others maneuvered for power, Constantine was a patron of scholarship and wrote books on various aspects of government. He was highly capable, however. Not only did he run an effective administration, he also inspired a cultural renaissance in the empire. He sponsored the recopying of ancient manuscripts, the writing of new reference works, and a revival of the study of science, mathematics, and literature. Constantine preferred law to war and left military matters to his generals, who made significant inroads into the Islamic states of Mesopotamia and Syria. After his father-in-law Romanus I was ousted from power, Constantine continued the efforts they had begun jointly to protect the tenants of small farms. He also maintained the contact that he and Romanus had established with the Russians, whom they hoped to convert to Christianity.

Constantine's successor, Romanus II, died in 963 CE after a short reign. His widow, Theophano, had the right to give her hand in marriage, and the crown with it, to the man of her choice. She chose Nicephorus Phocas, who had been Constantine's general and had commanded the army in the reconquest of Crete in 961 CE. Yet, in spite of his military successes, Nicephorus represented all the things that were detested by the cultured citizens of Constantinople. He was uneducated, coarse, and tyrannical. He also lived the life of an ascetic (without any luxuries). Ignoring all opposition, Nicephorus marched on the capital city, married Theophano, and ascended the imperial throne.

Nicephorus believed in the justice of the holy war against the Muslims. He put all the resources of the empire into the service of the military. Every Byzantine victory was followed almost at once by

The Byzantine emperors claimed that their authority was invested in them by God. This 10th-century-CE wood engraving depicts Christ crowning Constantine VII (ruled 913–959 CE).

fresh campaigns that required new recruits and new taxes.

Nicephorus considered the monasteries to be too rich for the good of their monks, so he decided to confiscate their property. That initiative antagonized the clergy, and relations between church and state deteriorated further when the emperor decreed that every Byzantine soldier killed in battle should be made a saint. In 969 CE, palace officials conspired against Nicephorus. They were aided by the empress Theophano, who had fallen in love with John Tzimisces (a companion-in-arms of the emperor) and wanted to marry him.

On the night of December 10, the conspirators, led by John Tzimisces, crept into the imperial bedchamber where the emperor (who rejected the comfort of the bed as a self-indulgence) lay asleep on the floor. They kicked him awake and then stabbed him to death.

The throne was then seized by John Tzimisces, who was forced by the patriarch of Constantinople to banish Theophano as a condition of his coronation. One of John's first acts was to intervene in Bulgaria (see box, page 1177) in 970 CE, with the result that Bulgaria became part of the Byzantine Empire. John also campaigned vigorously against the Islamic states in Mesopotamia and Syria from 972 to 975 CE. In 972 CE, John

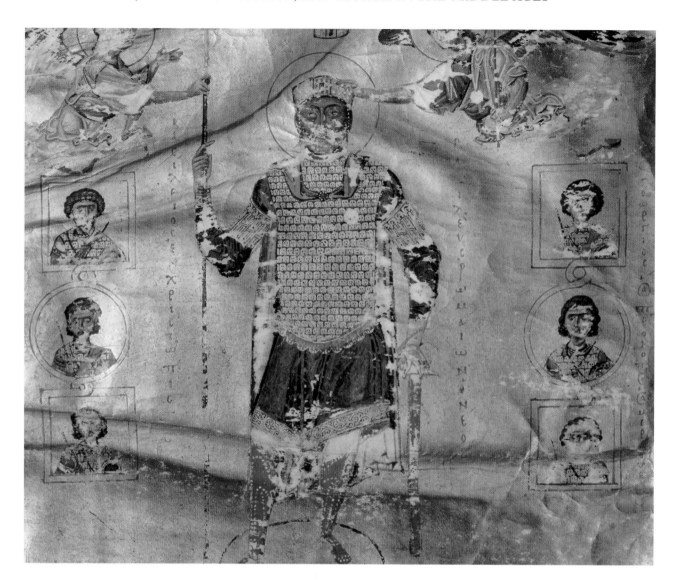

This illustration from the frontispiece of an 11th-century-CE Byzantine psalter (book of psalms) depicts the emperor Basil II subjugating the Bulgars.

arranged the marriage of Theophano to Otto, son of Henry I of Germany, in an effort to improve relations between the Byzantine and Holy Roman empires.

John Tzimisces died in 976 CE and was succeeded by Basil II, the son of Romanus II. Basil ruled jointly with his younger brother, Constantine VIII, who was happy to play a subordinate role in affairs of state. During Basil's reign, which lasted until 1025 CE, the Byzantine army regained territory in southeastern Anatolia, Greece, Macedonia, and Thrace. The Byzantine navy extended imperial power and established trading links in lands bordering the Mediterranean and Black seas.

Basil conquered Armenia, which was a threat to Byzantium from the east, and finally subdued the Bulgars, who, after the death of John Tzimisces, had claimed independence under the leadership of a self-proclaimed czar named Samuel. Basil waged war on the Bulgars for 20 years. He finally defeated Samuel in 1014 CE, and he owes his nickname, "the Bulgar slayer," to the savage way in which he dealt with the remnants of Samuel's army. The eyes of 15,000 Bulgarian prisoners were gouged out, although one soldier in every hundred was allowed to keep one eye in order to be able to lead the others home. In midwinter, Basil threw the blinded army out of the coun-

THE BULGARIAN EMPIRE

In the seventh century CE, Bulgar tribesmen of Turkic origin invaded Lower Moesia, a Balkan province of the Byzantine Empire. By the ninth century CE, they had formed their own empire, and their king, Khan Krum (ruled 803–814 CE), resoundingly defeated a Byzantine army in 811 CE and almost took Constantinople in 813 CE.

In 864 CE, Boris I (ruled 852–889 CE) was persuaded by the Byzantine emperor Michael III to make Christianity the official religion of Bulgaria. When, in 870 CE, Pope Adrian II refused to grant Bulgaria its own bishopric, Boris committed Bulgaria to Eastern Orthodoxy.

Boris's son, Simeon, brought Bulgaria to the zenith of its power through superb administration and successful military campaigns, most notably against the Byzantines and the Magyars. In 925 CE, Simeon declared himself czar of the Greeks as well as the Bulgars and went on to conquer Serbia the following year. However, he introduced Byzantine culture into his own empire and sponsored advances in education. His reign saw the first written works in the Bulgarian language and the adoption of the Cyrillic alphabet. Greatly influenced by its dominant Slavic population, Bulgaria became the center of Slavic culture in Europe during the 10th and 11th centuries CE.

After Simeon's death in 927 CE, Bulgaria's fortunes declined. In 970 CE, its capital and the royal family were captured by Russians. The Byzantine emperor John Tzimisces intervened, forcing the Russians out of the country. Although John promised to restore the young czar, Boris, to his throne, he had no intention of doing so. Soon after his successful campaign, John persuaded Boris to abdicate, and Bulgaria temporarily became a Byzantine province.

This 11th-century-CE manuscript illumination depicts Byzantine forces driving Bulgar cavalrymen away from the city of Thessaloniki.

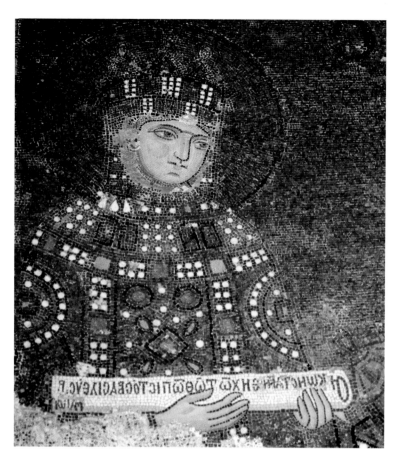

This 11th-century-CE mosaic from the Hagia Sophia in Constantinople (modern Istanbul) depicts the Byzantine empress Zoe.

death in 1041 CE, Zoe adopted Michael's nephew as her son and heir, and he was crowned Michael V. Trying to assert his authority, Michael had Zoe banished, a move that sparked a popular uprising. The empress was hastily re-called, but the mob was now out of con-trol, and Constantinople endured one of the bloodiest days in its history. Michael lost his throne and had his eyes gouged out.

Zoe married again. Her new hus-band, a high-ranking official, became Constantine IX. As emperor, Con-stantine's most striking characteristic was his indecisiveness. His death, in 1055 CE, heralded a period of upheaval.

The Battle of Manzikert

The 12 years following the death of Constantine IX saw a series of emper-ors. Then, on January 1, 1068 CE, an outstanding general was crowned as Romanus IV. The new *basileus* had been chosen partly because Constantinople's senior aristocrats and bureaucrats were alarmed by the weakness of the empire's armed forces in the face of new threats. Both on land and at sea, Byzantine strength had declined in the 11th cen-tury CE, while the very basis of the army—a regional network of units known as *themes*, each with its own leader—was failing to produce the num-ber of soldiers required, because the men had been allowed to buy their way out of service and work on farms instead.

The new threats faced by the empire came from the Normans in Italy and the Seljuk Turks, a central Asian people who had established an empire that included Iraq and much of Syria. In 1071 CE, Romanus IV mounted a large campaign to repel the Turks from eastern Anatolia. The two armies met near the town of Manzikert. During the ensuing battle, it seems likely that a large part of the Byzantine army was ordered to retreat as

try. When he saw his forces hobbling home, Samuel had a heart attack and died. Basil finally incorporated Bulgaria into the Byzantine Empire in 1018 CE.

The empress Zoe

Basil died in 1025 CE, leaving the Byzantine Empire in a strong position on all its frontiers. His aged brother, Constantine VIII, took over as sole ruler until his own death three years later. On his deathbed, Constantine sanctioned the marriage of his daughter Zoe to Romanus, the prefect of Constantin-ople. Within a few days, the two were crowned emperor and empress. The union was not a happy one, however. Romanus III took a mistress; the furious empress then had the emperor drowned in his bath. On the following day, she married her lover, the notorious pleasure-seeking Michael, making him emperor Michael IV. After Michael's part of a deliberate conspiracy. The withdrawal of troops left the vanguard, in which Romanus was fighting, unsupported. As the Turks attacked, the Byzantine line broke and their troops were massacred. Romanus was captured and taken to the camp of the Turkish commander, Alp Arslan, where he was treated courteously in accordance with Islamic rules of hospitality. A peace treaty was concluded, in which Romanus conceded some territories and agreed to pay a substantial ransom and an annual tribute. Romanus was then set free, but on his return to Constantinople, he was deposed by Michael VII, whose family may have conspired against Romanus at the Battle of Manzikert. Michael refused to honor the treaty with Alp Arslan, and the result was fresh incursions by the Turks, leading to the loss of much of Anatolia. Where the Turks did not conquer, they ravaged so thoroughly that the Anatolian population did not recover for more than a century, and the greatest recruiting ground for the empire's armies was laid to waste. The Battle of Manzikert had lasting repercussions and marked the beginning of the end of the Byzantine Empire.

The crusades

After the Battle of Manzikert, the Byzantine Empire was assailed on all sides by enemies and came close to ruin. It was saved, as it had been before, by the strength of the fortifications of Constantinople itself, which repelled successive waves of invaders, and by a brilliant military emperor, Alexius Comnenus (ruled 1081–1118 CE). Comnenus

This 14th-century-CE map depicts Constantinople at around the time of Marco Polo's visit to the city on his way from Venice to China (1252 CE).

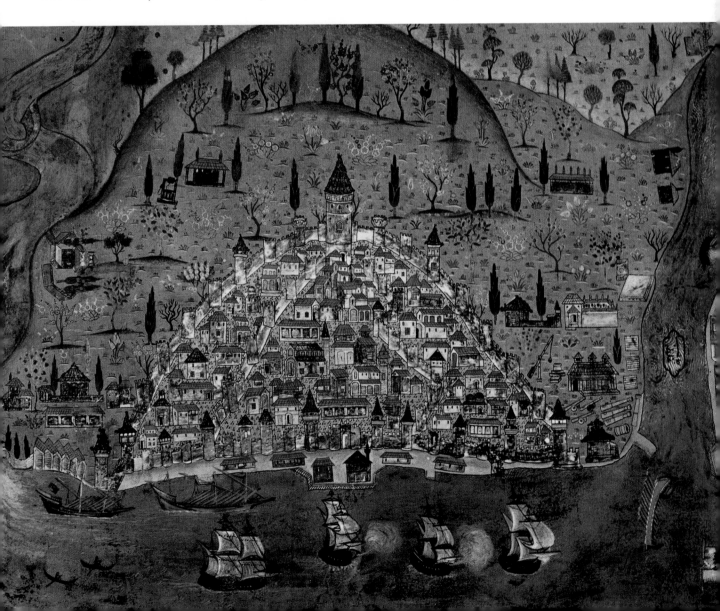

BYZANTINE ART OF THE MACEDONIAN RENAISSANCE

The end of iconoclasm in 847 CE heralded an outstanding period in Byzantine art as painters celebrated the new freedom of religious expression by producing a rich array of new icons, most of which were flat images produced with oil paint, mosaics, gold, and ivory.

Because it coincided with the Macedonian dynasty, this period in Byzantine art is known as the Macedonian Renaissance. Artists of the period returned to the classical Hellenistic style as the model for their paintings. However, because it was not acceptable to portray the naked human body in religious work, they adopted the Greek practice of clothing their figures in clinging drapery that merely hinted at the body beneath. The style is known as damp-fold. The artists also used abstract patterns or networks of lines to indicate the three-dimensional nature of their figures, rather than shading techniques that would have given a stronger sense of volume. Such artistic conventions—which were developed to conform with the requirements of the church—remained characteristic of Byzantine art for centuries.

Mosaic decoration followed a typical pattern that was closely linked to the predominant style of church architecture. Although broadly inspired by the structure of the famous Hagia Sophia in Constantinople (a great dome set over a square base), Middle Byzantine churches tended to be smaller and more intimate than their original models. While the earlier buildings had used huge curved arches (called pendentives) set on the sides of the square to support the domed roof, churches constructed during the Middle Byzantine period incorporated smaller arches (called squinches) at the corners of the square to hold the dome. The architects also added four equilateral areas to the sides of the square to form the arms of a cross. This cross-in-the-square became a common pattern, particularly in the 11th century CE.

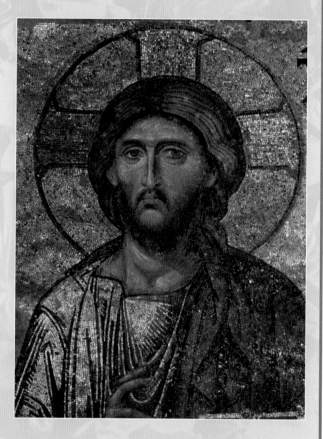

An outstanding example of Byzantine art of the Macedonian Renaissance, this mosaic from the Hagia Sophia depicts Jesus Christ.

The interior of most Byzantine churches was covered with mosaic or painted images of sacred people and events. Their position indicated the importance of the subject portrayed. Christ, always with a full beard, commanded the center of the dome, looking down on all creation. On the rim of the dome and high on the walls were biblical scenes and pictorial anecdotes from the life of the Virgin Mary, who was venerated as the mother of God. Important saints were shown on major structural supports, while less important ones appeared low down on the walls. In the semidome of the apse (a projection usually on the eastern side of the church), Mary was typically shown carrying the infant Jesus.

restored the empire's position in the Balkans by taking maximum advantage of the opportunities presented by the First Crusade. The defeat of Turkish forces by Christian knights enabled the emperor to reclaim many former Byzantine possessions in the region. Under Alexius Comnenus's two immediate successors—John Comnenus (ruled 1118–1143 CE) and Manuel Comnenus (ruled 1143–1180 CE)—Constantinople again exerted a major influence in the eastern Mediterranean. Exploiting limited resources to their full potential, the two emperors successfully played all their adversaries and rivals against each other. Their strategies enabled them to prevail against the Seljuk Turks in Anatolia, the crusader states in Palestine and Syria, the Normans in Italy, the maritime might of Venice in the Adriatic and the eastern Mediterranean, and the emerging powers of Bulgaria and Hungary in eastern Europe.

The Byzantine revival was brought to an end in 1185 CE, when the last of the Comnenus dynasty was deposed and murdered. The demise of the empire as a great power was now inevitable. The leaders of the Fourth Crusade agreed to a demand from the Venetians, who were transporting them to Palestine, that they attack Constantinople. The city, which had withstood so many attacks, was taken in 1204 CE and became the center of a new Latin empire that lasted for 57 years. Various Byzantine leaders formed states in other areas of the now much diminished empire.

After decades of warfare, Michael VIII reestablished the Byzantine Empire in 1261 CE by recapturing Constantinople from his original base in Nicaea. However, the state was now a mere shadow of its former self. It survived only by allying itself with the Turkish states in Anatolia and by agreeing to their sovereignty over it. By 1350 CE, the Byzantine

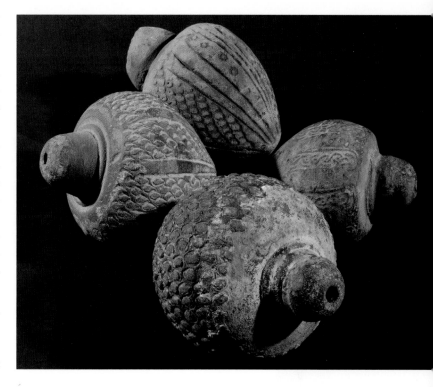

Empire consisted of no more than Constantinople itself, Thessaloniki, and parts of southern Greece. Although Constantinople repelled sieges by the Ottoman Turks in 1398–1399 CE and 1422 CE, the city was unable to withstand a further Ottoman onslaught in 1453 CE.

The last Byzantine emperor, Constantine XI, made every effort to salvage the situation; he even tried to forge an alliance with western Christendom by pledging allegiance to the church of Rome. Help was not forthcoming, however, and Constantine was killed in 1453 CE while attempting, unsuccessfully, to repel the Turks from the walls of the city that had once dominated the eastern Mediterranean. The final tiny remnant of the Byzantine Empire, the port of Trebizond on the Black Sea, was conquered by the Ottomans in 1461 CE.

These terra-cotta hand grenades were among the weapons in the Byzantine arsenal during the unsuccessful defense of Constantinople against Ottoman Turkish forces in 1453 CE.

See also:

The Age of Charlemagne (volume 6, page 788) • The Caliphate (volume 6, page 764) • The Early Byzantine Empire (volume 9, page 1158)

THE CRUSADES

The crusades were a series of Christian military expeditions that aimed to capture the Holy Land—particularly Jerusalem—from Muslim rule. Although they were never entirely successful, the crusades preoccupied Europeans for more than 250 years.

From 1095 CE, when Pope Urban II (ruled 1088–1099 CE) proclaimed the First Crusade, medieval Europe launched a series of Holy Wars. Most of these military campaigns were aimed at taking the holy places in Palestine away from Muslim control, but some of them were directed against the Muslims in Spain. Other crusades targeted pagan peoples of eastern Europe, while the Albigensian Crusade (see box, page 1194) tried to root out heresy in southern France.

At the heart of the crusades lay a deep religious impulse that seldom manifested itself benevolently. More commonly, the crusades were characterized by enormous savagery toward non-Christians (and sometimes other Christians), and they were always overlaid by the personal and political ambitions of their leaders. The crusades also had social causes. Rising population levels and the need for the younger sons of nobles to establish their own fiefdoms are widely regarded as two of the main reasons why many Europeans found interest in the Holy Wars. The crusades had no single main cause; there were many complex reasons for them.

The First Crusade

The First Crusade was proclaimed in 1095 CE by Pope Urban II at the Council of Clermont, a city in France.

There were two ostensible reasons for the Pope's announcement. The first reason was that Christian pilgrims were encountering problems in the Holy Land. Pilgrimage had become an important part of religious life by the late 11th century CE, but Palestine was under the control of Seljuk Turks who made Christians unwelcome in Jerusalem. The second reason was related to the split that had happened between the eastern and western Christian churches in 1054 CE. In 1071 CE, the Seljuks defeated Byzantine forces at the Battle of Manzikert and threatened Constantinople itself. The Byzantine emperor Alexius Comnenus then called on western Christendom for help. Alexius worked on detente with the Latin Christians, and Urban was anxious to restore relations between the two churches. As a result, Urban finally rescinded the excommunication under which Rome had held Byzantium since the original schism. In return, Alexius reopened the Latin churches in Constantinople.

Pope Urban II was keen on providing armed assistance, which he saw as a means for reuniting the whole Christian church while reclaiming the Holy Land for Christendom. At Clermont, he out-

This illuminated manuscript from the 15th century CE depicts Pope Urban II addressing the Council of Clermont in 1095 CE.

austres saine lieuz la environ.
t les ypiens phabitans z demou
ns. z que les austres par eulx
zranniquement z Inhumaine
ent tues. Ils auoient referue
Infeliciense bie a fin que sur
lby en lopprobre du saint nom
iens peussent continuer plus
uquement leurs Insatiables

ainaultes. Et comment Ils
les tenoient en trop oprobrieuse
captiuite z seruage. ou tresgrant
deshonneur z oprobre de tous
les ypiens. Concluant z mou
strant par diuerses raisons tres
euidentes que le saint peuple
ypien ne debuoit plus souffrir
nenduret que les sains lieuz et

KEY SITES FROM THE CRUSADES

Zara
Nis
Black Sea
Bari
Constantinople
Nicaea
Dorylaeum
ANATOLIA
Edessa
SYRIA
Antioch
Aleppo
RHODES
CYPRUS
Tripoli
Damascus
Acre
Hattin
PALESTINE
Mediterranean Sea
Jerusalem
Alexandria
Damietta
Nile
EGYPT

KEY

✕ Major battle

lined his plan for a war to end Muslim control over Jerusalem. Urban appealed to Christians to turn their warrior spirit to a holy cause. He called the war a crusade, taking the name from the Latin word *crux* (cross). His proposal was immediately acclaimed. "*Deus le vult*" (God wills it!), shouted the vast crowd assembled in a field outside Clermont.

Answering the call to arms

The first bishop to respond to the pope's challenge was Adhemar of Le Puy (France). Almost immediately, several hundred people followed Adhemar's example and pledged themselves to the cause. The pope appointed Adhemar commander in chief of the First Crusade and directed the other bishops to return home and start recruiting. The idea was that groups of crusaders, each with their own leader and financing, would converge on Constantinople and join forces with the Byzantines. Together, they would retake Anatolia (part of modern Turkey) from the Seljuks and then proceed to Syria and Palestine.

Throughout Europe, the popular response to Urban's call was enthusiastic. The enlistment effort began at once. It largely followed the pope's plan, but Urban had not anticipated the excitement it would arouse among the common people of Europe. Peasants and city folk, merchants and adventurers alike sewed crosses on their clothing and joined in what became known as the People's Crusade.

The largest popular army was recruited and led by a preacher from northern France named Peter the Hermit (c. 1050–1115 CE). Peter assembled an undisciplined mob of some 40,000 people in France and Germany. With no equipment and few provisions, they set off eastward, plundering as they went. In Hungary, they attacked the town of Semlin, killing many of its inhabitants. Their onward rampage continued with many skirmishes until Byzantine troops were sent to oppose them at Nis (a city in modern Serbia) and many crusaders were killed. The Christian forces reached Constantinople in August of 1096 CE with their numbers greatly reduced.

Alexius Comnenus was horrified by this response to his appeal for help. It was clear to him that this rabble army could not remain in the city, where it had already begun to plunder and rape. Alexius arranged for the army to be shipped to Anatolia, where it marched straight into a Turkish ambush. Most of the crusaders were killed, and the survivors were sold into slavery.

Crusaders against Jews

The crusaders' recruitment drive in the Rhineland met with particular success. Large numbers of Christians accepted the pilgrim's cross, but the armies in which they enlisted fell into the hands of profiteering robber barons. They were further distracted from their mission to the Holy Land by potential targets much closer to home. They turned against the Jews, who were persecuted because they had not been baptized.

After plundering Jewish possessions, the Christian army of the Rhineland headed east in the wake of Peter the Hermit. They did not get far, however. Having learned from experience what a

crusading army could do, the Hungarian king closed his borders to the invaders, who then dispersed. Many of them died before they could return home.

Regular armies

More suited to what Urban II had intended were five independent armies that formed in 1096 CE. Drawn primarily from France, these forces also included recruits from Flanders, Lorraine, Burgundy, and southern Italy. Following the pope's plan, they intended to converge on Constantinople, from where the whole crusade would proceed to the Holy Land.

The first (and smallest) of these armies was led by Hugh of Vermandois, brother of Philip I of France. Another French army was commanded by Robert of Flanders, who marched his troops into Italy and then sailed from Bari to the Holy Land. Raymond of Toulouse led the largest contingent, 10,000 men, who

This 12th-century-CE Byzantine gold coin bears the image of the emperor Alexius Comnenus.

POPE URBAN II

The man who eventually became Urban II was born Odo of Lagery in France around 1040 CE. He became prior of the Benedictine monastery at Cluny in 1072 CE, and then he was elected to the office of pope in 1088 CE. During his term as the pope, Urban continued the Cluniac reforms that had been introduced by his predecessors. Urban's particular concerns were ending the schism with the Byzantine Christians and reclaiming the Holy Land from the Muslims.

Urban was delighted when the Byzantine emperor Alexius Comnenus appealed to him for help in recovering Anatolia from the Seljuk Turks. In initiating the Holy War, Urban felt that relations between eastern and western Christianity would be strengthened as soldiers fought side by side against the common enemy of their faith and that by serving in the Holy War soldiers would improve their own chances of personal salvation. Urban died in 1099 CE.

This portrait of Pope Urban II was painted by the Spanish artist Francisco de Zurbarán (1598–1664 CE).

marched from Lyon, across the top of Italy, and down the northern shore of the Adriatic Sea. Godfrey of Bouillon traveled through Hungary, where, because his troops were more disciplined than the peasant army, he encountered less resistance from the Hungarian king. The last army was led by Bohemond of Taranto, the eldest son of Robert Guiscard, a longtime enemy of Byzantium. The First Crusade had no overall commander. The leaders of the various contingents had to agree on a course of action. They were fortunate that Bishop Adhemar proved a formidable diplomat and kept them together during their first campaigns. However, he died in 1098 CE, shortly after the siege of Antioch.

In November of 1096 CE, the Christian armies began arriving in Constantinople. The crusaders were not warmly welcomed. After dispatching the rabble army of Peter the Hermit, the city now treated all crusaders with suspicion. Alexius was particularly skeptical of the motives of the leaders. He suspected that they were hoping to conquer Byzantine lands for themselves, and he insisted that each leader swear allegiance to him. The crusaders were unwilling to do so, but the emperor was powerful enough to put pressure on each one in turn. In addition, Alexius required that they should return to him any former Byzantine lands they conquered. Once the oath was sworn, each new vassal was ferried with his army across the Bosporus before the next army arrived.

The conquest of Anatolia

In May of 1097 CE, the crusaders began their first coordinated campaign in Anatolia, besieging the Seljuk stronghold of Nicaea. The city surrendered in June (mainly due to astute negotiation by Alexius Comnenus, who, to the disappointment of the crusader leaders, agreed that the city should not be sacked). The

city's surrender came not a day too soon for the crusaders, who were suffering from a severe shortage of food. Their plight was exacerbated as the campaign continued, because the Turks operated a scorched-earth policy, burning crops and stores as they retreated.

On July 1, 1097 CE, the crusaders won a resounding victory over the Turks at the Battle of Dorylaeum. Although the Christians were outmaneuvered at first, a sudden cavalry charge by heavily armored crusader knights shattered the Turks. The invaders then moved on to the ancient city of Antioch (in northern Syria), which they besieged in October. They managed to enter the city, but they were then trapped by a relief

This 15th-century-CE illustration depicts Godfrey of Bouillon, one of the leading warriors of the First Crusade. Bouillon is a town in modern Belgium.

This medieval painting depicts the siege of Antioch during the First Crusade.

force while the citadel of Antioch held out against them.

Many rank-and-file crusaders were given fresh hope when a priest from southern France claimed to have had a dream in which Saint Andrew showed him the location of the lance used to pierce Christ's side and told him that whoever possessed this relic would be invincible. There was considerable dispute about the meaning of the vision, but the crusaders eventually left the city and defeated the relief force. The emir in the citadel then surrendered, and most of his warriors agreed to be baptized as Christians.

After the surrender of Antioch, the crusaders spent the next few months ravaging the surrounding countryside and squabbling over who should control the city. The Byzantine claim to Antioch was forgotten, and many of the crusading nobles wanted to claim it for themselves, following the example of Godfrey of Bouillon's brother, Baldwin, who had seized Edessa and created his own state. Antioch was eventually awarded to Bohemond as a county (a region ruled by a count). The city remained in the hands of his descendants until 1268 CE.

Reaching Jerusalem

In November of 1098 CE, Raymond of Toulouse led his crusader forces south, and the other leaders, with the exception of Bohemond, followed him. They entered territory controlled not by the Seljuk Turks but by the Fatimid rulers of Egypt, who had taken Jerusalem from the Turks in August of 1098 CE. In June of

1099 CE, the exhausted crusader army pitched camp at the gates of Jerusalem. After a solemn pilgrimage to the Jordan River, and after acquiring fresh supplies from a Genoese fleet, the crusaders constructed siege towers and attacked the city. On July 15, they succeeded in taking a section of the city wall and opening a gate. The Fatimid governor surrendered and was given safe conduct out of the city, but the crusader forces then massacred all the Muslim and Jewish inhabitants of Jerusalem. A Fatimid relief force was driven off, and having achieved their goal, many of the crusaders returned home to Europe.

Godfrey of Bouillon was elected to rule Jerusalem and the conquered territories around it. He chose not to be called king, because, as he said, he did not want a golden crown when "Christ had worn a thorny crown." Instead, he took the title "Protector of the Holy Sepulchre." Godfrey died after only a year in office, and his brother, Baldwin of Edessa, was chosen to succeed him. Having no objection to a coronation, Baldwin became the first king of Jerusalem.

In the immediate aftermath of the capture of Jerusalem, several crusader states were formed: the county of Edessa in the north, the principality of Antioch, the county of Tripoli, and the kingdom of Jerusalem itself. These crusader states were always precarious. They remained enclaves in Muslim territory and were constantly in danger of attack. The success of the First Crusade was the result not so much of the strength of the Christian armies but of the weakness of the Muslims. The Seljuks had been split into several different states while they were at war with the Fatimids of Egypt. Strong Muslim rulers could easily make inroads, as the Seljuk leader Imad ad-Din Zangi did in 1144 CE, when, from his base in Mosul (a city in modern Iraq), he took the county of Edessa.

The Second Crusade

After Jerusalem was taken by the crusaders in 1099 CE, the kingdom of Jerusalem was able to maintain itself as one of a number of small competing Christian and Muslim states in the region. Its rulers faced a constant man-

Originally an Arab fortress, Krak des Chevaliers, in modern Syria, fell to the crusaders in 1099 CE. The castle later became the headquarters of the Knights Hospitaller.

This 15th-century-CE manuscript illumination depicts the siege of Damascus by the armies of the Second Crusade in 1148 CE.

power shortage, however, because there were insufficient Christian settlers to form the basis of a large feudal-style army. The kingdom's defenses relied heavily on the warrior monks of two orders, the Knights Templar and the Knights Hospitaller, whose ranks had to be constantly replenished by new recruits from Europe. Thus, when a strong leader emerged to unite the various Muslim states of Syria and northern Iraq, the Christian states were in grave danger.

The leader in question was Imad ad-Din Zangi, the ruler of the territories of Mosul and Aleppo (a city in modern Syria). Under his leadership, the Muslims were able to reconquer Edessa in 1144 CE and then threaten the kingdom of Jerusalem itself.

The crusaders in Jerusalem sent an urgent plea for help to the pope, Eugenius III (ruled 1145–1153 CE), and in 1145 CE, the pope called for a new crusade to relieve the Holy City. King Louis VII of France and Conrad, the Holy Roman emperor, both raised armies and departed for Palestine, passing through Constantinople on the way. As had happened half a century earlier with the First Crusade, the armies, particularly the Germans, were undisciplined and caused havoc as they passed through Byzantine territory.

The armies, understandably, were not popular with the Byzantines by the time they reached Constantinople, and the Byzantine emperor quickly sent them on their way. The German army was ambushed and cut to pieces by Turkish forces near Dorylaeum in 1147 CE. Only a small number of the French crusaders managed to reach Palestine, where they made a strategic error. They decided not to attack the Turks who had conquered Edessa; instead, the crusaders targeted Damascus, which was nearer but was also an independent city-state that could have been an ally, because it was also being threatened by the Turks.

In July of 1148 CE, the crusaders mounted a wave of assaults on Damascus, but its walls were strong and the attackers were repelled over and over. After only five days of fighting, the crusaders withdrew, and the remnants of their armies returned home to Europe. The fiasco of the Second Crusade was over.

Saladin

Pressure mounted on the kingdom of Jerusalem under Zangi's successor, Nur ad-Din, who developed his realm into a major power. Commanded by the legendary Saladin (c. 1138–1193 CE), Nur ad-Din's forces conquered Egypt in 1169 CE. After Nur ad-Din's death in 1174 CE, Saladin took over, vowing to recapture Jerusalem for the Muslim faith. Saladin's forces, in control of both Syria and Egypt, almost surrounded the crusader states. Having allowed a truce with Saladin to be broken, Guy de Lusignan, king of Jerusalem (ruled 1186–1194 CE), was crushingly defeated in 1187 CE at the

Battle of Hattin, around 20 miles (32 km) west of the Sea of Galilee. In October, Saladin occupied Jerusalem and allowed Christian inhabitants to leave unharmed after paying a ransom.

This 15th-century-CE portrait depicts the great Muslim warrior Saladin.

POPE INNOCENT III

Innocent III was born in 1160 CE to a leading Italian family in Rome. He was well educated and ambitious. Due to family connections, he was made pope in 1198 CE at the age of 37. He was one of the most worldly and politically minded popes, and during his reign, the papacy achieved its greatest influence over the monarchs of Europe. In some cases, kings actually had to swear fealty to Innocent.

Innocent's dream was to see Jerusalem freed from Muslim control, and in 1202 CE, he inaugurated the Fourth Crusade. Although the expedition ended in failure, the pope did not give up; less than a year before his death, he extracted a promise from the young German emperor, Frederick II, that he would lead another crusade to liberate the Holy City.

The pope's religious fervor also had results closer to home. In 1209 CE, Innocent instigated a crusade against the Albigensians in southern France, declaring that heresy was "treason against God" and that it must be rooted out at all costs. Innocent did not live to see the outcome of this crusade; he died in 1216 CE.

The Third Crusade

Pope Gregory VIII called for a Third Crusade in October of 1187 CE. The expedition was eventually led by the French king Philip II, the Holy Roman emperor Frederick I, and the English king Richard I. They commanded the largest army of crusaders since 1096 CE, but they did not retake Jerusalem. Frederick died before reaching the Holy Land, and his soldiers returned to Germany. Philip and Richard succeeded in securing a number of cities on the Mediterranean, reestablishing a small Latin kingdom (based in the port of Acre) that lasted for a century. Although the Third Crusade failed to achieve its objective, it was more successful than those that followed it.

The Fourth Crusade

In 1198 CE, the new pope, Innocent III (see box, page 1191), called for another crusade to recapture the Holy City. The venture got off to a bad start. In 1202

CE, the crusaders joined with Venetian forces who wanted to recapture Zara (modern Zadar, Croatia) from the Hungarians. When the pope heard of the diversion, he was furious and excommunicated the whole expedition. The crusaders then joined forces with a claimant to the Byzantine throne and seized Constantinople on his behalf. However, once the emperor had been reinstated, he refused to pay for their services. The crusaders then considered themselves justified in plundering the city, which they did with appalling brutality.

After sacking Constantinople, the crusaders installed their own emperor, Count Baldwin of Flanders, whose coronation as Baldwin I in May of 1204 CE initiated a period of Latin rule over Byzantium. In 1228 CE, Baldwin II inherited the throne at the age of 11. John of Brienne, a former king of Jerusalem, took over as regent, and Baldwin spent much of his adult life in Europe, trying to gather an army to

This illustration from around 1400 CE depicts the reconquest of Jerusalem by Saladin in 1187 CE.

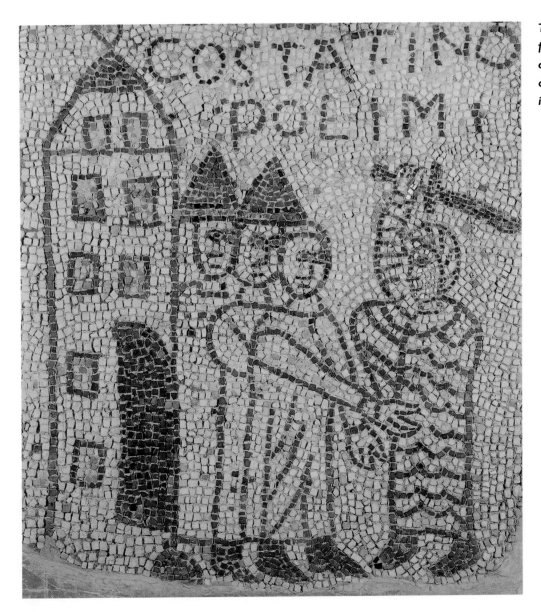

recover the parts of his empire that had been seized by the Bulgarians and Greeks. Latin rule ended in 1261 CE, when Baldwin lost Constantinople to the Byzantine emperor Michael VIII.

The Fifth Crusade

Rather than targeting Jerusalem, the Fifth Crusade was directed toward Egypt. This was one of the least successful crusades. In 1219 CE, the Christian warriors captured the Egyptian port of Damietta, but the reinforcements that they needed and expected never materialized. The crusaders failed to take Cairo and were forced to hand Damietta back in 1221 CE. After that loss, the crusaders retreated to Europe.

Later crusades

Frederick II had vowed in 1215 CE and again in 1220 CE that he would lead a crusade to the Holy Land, and Pope Gregory IX was anxious to make the emperor keep his promise. Frederick finally set sail in 1227 CE, but an epidemic forced him to return to port. The pope promptly excommunicated the emperor. A year later, Frederick sailed to Egypt and negotiated with the Egyptian

THE ALBIGENSIAN CRUSADE

The major crusade fought in Europe was proclaimed in 1209 CE by Pope Innocent III against the Albigenses, a heretical sect based in Carcassonne and the surrounding region of Languedoc in southern France.

The Albigenses were Cathars, a group that held there was a god of good competing with a separate god of evil. The god of goodness and light was identified with Jesus Christ and the God in the New Testament of the Bible. The god of evil and darkness was identified with the devil and the God in the Old Testament. The Cathars believed in reincarnation and that the only way to escape being reborn as a person or an animal was to lead a good life on earth; such a life would be rewarded with a spiritual existence after death.

This 14th-century-CE painting depicts the expulsion of Albigenses from Carcassonne.

Cathars lived either as simple believers (who led ordinary lives) or as perfects (ascetics). The perfects were believed to be able to commune with God in prayer; they were strict vegetarians and were not allowed possessions or sexual relations. Simple believers could become perfects through a rite called *consolamentum* (consolation), a "laying on of hands" that was frequently administered just before death.

The Albigensian heresy had a political aspect, because the Cathars regarded the Roman Catholic Church, with all its corruption, wealth, and interest in material power, as the agent of the devil. In the first period of the crusade against the Albigenses, Simon de Montfort the Elder (c. 1165–1218 CE) led an army of around 10,000 knights from France and Burgundy to combat the heretical forces under the count of Toulouse, whose ancestor, Raymond of Toulouse, had led the largest contingent on the First Crusade.

The first phase of the Albigensian Crusade was ended in 1229 CE by the Treaty of Paris. The heresy remained, however, and soon provoked a second period of hostilities, which lasted until around 1271 CE. Captured heretics were handed over to the Inquisition, which tortured them in an effort to force them to renounce their beliefs. Many, however, preferred death to dishonor. On one occasion, in 1244 CE, some 200 Cathars were burned alive on a great pyre in the town of Montségur.

Because the property of the Cathars and their sympathizers was confiscated, the Albigensian Crusade brought a large territory in southern France under the control of the French crown. The Albigensian heresy was not fully crushed until the 14th century CE.

sultan Al Kamil, who surrendered Jerusalem to the emperor in 1229 CE and signed a 10-year peace treaty.

Jerusalem again proved difficult to defend, and in 1244 CE, the city fell to Turkish and Egyptian forces. In Europe, there was a flurry of interest in a crusade to recapture the Holy City. Louis IX of France spent years planning a campaign before he sailed from Cyprus and captured Damietta in June of 1249 CE. However, his attempt on Cairo the following spring was defeated when the Egyptians opened reservoir sluice gates along the Nile River, trapping the French army and forcing Louis to surrender in April of 1250 CE. The king paid a ransom to secure his own release and was forced to hand back Damietta. He then sailed for Palestine, where he spent four years helping to improve the defenses of the Latin kingdom.

Back in France, Louis tried in 1270 CE to mobilize support for another crusade against the city of Tunis. The French nobility was unsupportive, but Louis carried on regardless and died in Tunisia the same year.

The remaining crusader strongholds in western Asia fell one by one to the new rulers of Egypt—the Mamluk dynasty. Acre succumbed in May of 1291 CE, and its Christian occupiers fled first to Cyprus and then to Rhodes. Although the Europeans made further sporadic attempts to regain lost territory—including a Cyprus-based attack on Alexandria, Egypt, in 1365 CE—the crusades had run their course.

Later popes sometimes preached crusades in an effort to slow the advance of the Ottoman Turks into western Europe in the 15th and 16th centuries CE, but their initiatives were defensive and quite unlike the confident, expansionist calls to arms that had first energized Europe and inspired the masses in the 11th century CE.

Some of the Christian warriors who fled Acre in 1291 CE settled permanently on the Greek island of Rhodes. There they built walled fortifications such as this in the crusader style.

See also:

The Middle and Late Byzantine Empire (volume 9, page 1168) • Popes and Emperors (volume 8, page 1058) • The Reconquista and Christian Expansion (volume 8, page 1014) • Rulers of the 13th Century (volume 8, page 1070)

THE VIKINGS

The Vikings sailed in longships from their native Scandinavia to plunder and sometimes to colonize large areas of the Northern Hemisphere. Their influence extended from the shores of the Black Sea to the eastern seaboard of North America.

From the 8th to the 11th century CE, the coasts of northern Europe were attacked repeatedly by Viking raiders. The Vikings were pagans from Scandinavia, and for around 400 years, they sailed the seas and rivers of Europe in their longships, plundering villages and monasteries, taking towns, creating their own principalities, and holding whole countries for ransom.

At home in Denmark, Norway, and Sweden, the Vikings—sometimes known alternatively as Norsemen—were farmers, fishermen, or merchants. Their longships enabled them to buy and sell in distant countries. They traded in furs, precious metals, and foodstuffs such as dried herrings, but above all, they traded in slaves. The very name of the Slav peoples of eastern Europe comes from the word *slave*, because so many Slavs were captured and sold into slavery by the Vikings.

Attacks on England

Some Vikings set out by sea from their homelands with the specific intention of raiding and plundering. Their principal targets were Christian communities in England and elsewhere that had monasteries laden with wealth and completely undefended.

In June of 793 CE, a party of Vikings attacked and sacked the monastery of Lindisfarne, an island off the northeastern coast of England. The monks were either killed or taken prisoner to be sold as slaves; the monastery was destroyed, and everything of value was looted. The event sent shockwaves through the Christian world. The Lindisfarne raid was the first of many similar attacks on monasteries and isolated communities as the Viking marauders targeted the islands around Scotland and Ireland.

By the second half of the ninth century CE, Viking ships were regularly plundering the eastern and southern coasts of England, where they encountered little effective resistance. England at that time was divided into four main kingdoms—Northumbria in the north, East Anglia in the east, Mercia in the midlands, and Wessex in the south. The kingdoms were rivals and often at war with each other; united opposition to the common enemy was therefore impractical. When the Viking raiders appeared, the local inhabitants simply fled.

In 865 CE, three Viking brothers—Halfdan, Ivar the Boneless, and Ubbi—landed an armed force in East Anglia and marched north to Eboracum (modern York). They captured the ancient Roman

Known as Sigurd's Helmet, this seventh-century-CE Viking head protector was recovered from a buried longship in Sweden.

city, which was then the capital of Northumbria, and turned it into a mighty fortress of their own.

The Viking force in Eboracum became known as the Great Army. It fought off two Northumbrian lords and secured the whole of Northumbria. Ivar then headed south to East Anglia, where he defeated and killed the local king. The Vikings, in possession of two of the English kingdoms, also made inroads into Mercia. They were then content to settle for what they had won, and most of them reverted to their original occupation as farmers.

The ruined monastery of Lindisfarne is still a reminder of the Viking attack on it in 793 CE, which heralded the start of the Viking Age.

In 871 CE, another Viking leader, Guthrum, attacked Wessex. The new king of Wessex, Alfred the Great (ruled 871–899 CE), made a determined stand against the invaders. Hostilities continued for several years, and then, around 878 CE, the two sides signed a treaty that recognized the right of the Vikings to settle in northeastern England. Because most of the Vikings who took part in the invasion were Danes, the area became known as the Danelaw. Under the terms of the treaty, Guthrum also agreed to be baptized as a Christian.

The struggle between the Vikings and the English was far from over, however. Despite Alfred's efforts to protect Wessex, the Vikings remained entrenched in much of northern and eastern England, and during the 10th and early 11th centuries CE, Scandinavian campaigns to capture Wessex intensified. In 1013 CE, Sweyn Forkbeard (the overlord of Norway, Sweden, and Denmark) arrived in northern England with a great army, and the established inhabitants of the Danelaw swore allegiance to him. Marching southward, Forkbeard's forces so intimidated the English that many abandoned the Wessex king, Aethelred the Unready (ruled 978–1016 CE), and

THE VIKING WORLD

ICELAND

FAROE ISLANDS

SHETLAND ISLANDS

NORWAY

SWEDEN

• Novgorod

SCOTLAND

North Sea

GOTLAND

Lindisfarne •

DENMARK

Baltic Sea

NORTHUMBRIA

MERCIA

• Eboracum (York)

WESSEX

EAST ANGLIA

• Kiev

Dnieper River

Volga River

NORMANDY

• Rouen

Chartres •

• Paris

Tours •

BURGUNDY

Atlantic Ocean

Black Sea

ITALY

• Constantinople

Mediterranean Sea SICILY

joined forces with the Scandinavians. Aethelred fled to Normandy, and Forkbeard claimed the whole of England as his own. Forkbeard's triumph was short-lived, however; he died suddenly only a few weeks later, leaving his new kingdom to his son, Cnut (or Canute).

The transfer of power from Sweyn Forkbeard to Cnut was not smooth. Aethelred returned from exile with a new army, and Cnut had to fight for his inheritance. However, Aethelred and his son Edmund Ironside both died in 1016 CE, and Cnut became undisputed king of the whole of England, which he ruled until his death in 1035 CE. Cnut held sway over a vast empire that consisted of England, Norway, Denmark, and some of what is now Sweden.

The Vikings in France

At the beginning of the ninth century CE, the emperor Charlemagne (ruled 800–814 CE) was the most powerful monarch in Europe, presiding over a vast Carolingian Empire that included much of France, Germany, the Netherlands, and northern Italy. However, his lands were not immune to the northern raiders. In 810 CE, some 200 Danish longships raided the coast of Frisia and demanded tribute. In the 840s CE, the Danes sacked the Frankish towns of Rouen, Chartres, and Tours; by the middle of the ninth century CE, extensive areas of France were effectively in Danish hands. In late 885 CE, an army of 30,000 Danes, carried in 700 longships, sailed up the Seine River and laid siege to Paris.

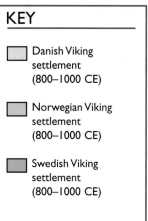

KEY

Danish Viking settlement (800–1000 CE)

Norwegian Viking settlement (800–1000 CE)

Swedish Viking settlement (800–1000 CE)

This 14th-century-CE illuminated manuscript features a portrait of King Cnut.

Following their repeated raids into northern France, the Danish Vikings eventually settled permanently in the region. At the beginning of the 10th century CE, their leader, Rollo, agreed a treaty with the Frankish king, Charles the Simple (ruled 893–922 CE). Rollo undertook to swear allegiance to Charles and to defend the territory then known as Neustria (modern Normandy) on behalf of Charles. Rollo became duke of Normandy in 911 CE, and he agreed to become a Christian. His warriors were all granted land and settled down into a feudal society. The Normans then entered an era of expansionism that brought them, in 1066 CE, the throne of England and, later, their own state in southern Italy and Sicily. Norman knights also played an important role in the First Crusade.

Vikings in the east

Unlike the Danish and Norwegian Vikings, who sailed southward and westward, the Swedish Vikings directed their expeditions eastward across the Baltic Sea into lands that gave them access to the rivers of eastern Europe. From the early ninth century CE, Swedish Vikings made regular raids across the region, exacting tributes from the Slavic nobles and enslaving large numbers of ordinary people. They then established a trade route from their homelands, across eastern Europe, and south into the Byzantine, Arab, and Turkish states of the eastern Mediterranean and western Asia. The prosperity of this commercial artery is evidenced by the discovery, in 2006 CE, of more than one thousand Arab silver coins buried on the Swedish island of Gotland in the Baltic Sea.

However, they failed to capture the city. After weeks of fighting and serious casualties on both sides, the Frankish king, Charles the Fat (ruled 876–888 CE), arrived with troops and made a deal with the Danes. In return for a sum of money and free passage out of the area, the Danes agreed to lift the siege, sail farther inland, and help Charles to put down an uprising by the people of Burgundy.

The Swedish traders and raiders gradually took over the Slavic tribes of the eastern Baltic coast. A semilegendary leader named Rurik established himself at Novgorod (a city in modern Russia).

Two other Viking leaders, Askold and Dir, pressed on along the Dnieper River to Kiev, almost 600 miles (960 km) to the south.

Kiev later became a vital link on the prosperous trade route between Scandinavia and Constantinople. In 860 CE, a Viking force of 200 longships completed a foray along the whole length of the Dnieper River and reached Constantinople itself. Realizing immediately that they would be unable to take the city, the Vikings instead plundered the surrounding villages and monasteries, slaughtering the inhabitants without mercy. They sailed away laden with booty.

The leaders of that expedition were the rulers of Kiev, Askold and Dir. Oleg, who had gained power in Novgorod after Rurik's death, quickly decided that the continued division of power in the region was unsatisfactory. Oleg invited Askold and Dir to a meeting, claiming that he wanted to make joint plans for the future, but when they arrived, he had them both murdered. Oleg became supreme ruler of the new state, known as Kievan Rus.

According to a 12th-century-CE account, another Viking expedition set out for Constantinople around 907 CE. It was a substantial force of 80,000 men in 2,000 ships, under the command of Oleg. Already involved in a war with the Bulgars in the Balkans, the Byzantine emperor agreed to talk terms with the Vikings. He paid a large tribute and, more important, ratified a trade agreement that allowed the Vikings to enter the city for the purpose of trade.

Oleg now controlled an immensely lucrative trade route, from Constantinople to the Baltic Sea, but he was still not satisfied. The Vikings penetrated the lands of the Khazars, the region between the

This 19th-century-CE engraving depicts the siege of Paris by Vikings in 885 CE.

THE VIKING LONGSHIP

The success of the Viking raids depended on their longships, which were fast, sturdily built warships. A typical longship was around 60–80 feet (18–24 m) from stem to stern, a narrow boat constructed from overlapping oak planks. It had a shallow keel, which allowed it to navigate rivers, and it was powered by sail and oars.

There were around 30 oarsmen on each side of a ship. Rowing together, they could propel the vessel in calm weather conditions, while a large, rectangular cloth sail enabled the ship to sail in favorable breezes at up to 10 knots (11.5 mph; 18.5 km/h). At that speed, the Vikings could cross from Norway to England in 24 hours.

On the prow of each warship was a carved dragon's head, the appearance of which was calculated to inspire fear in all who saw it. The longship's sails were often brightly colored to draw attention to the fleet. When sailing on a hostile raid, the warriors often hung their shields along the outside of the ship's hull.

The Vikings were excellent navigators, which enabled them to make their hair-raising crossings of the Atlantic Ocean. They navigated by the sun and stars, and they may have had help from a mysterious sunstone, a crystal that polarized light. Despite the fact that their vessels were oceangoing, they were also light enough to be hauled overland when necessary, such as, for example, on unnavigable stretches of the Dnieper River during the advance to Kiev in the ninth century CE. The Vikings placed their ships on tree trunks, which were used as rollers.

As a reminder of the Viking Age, replica longships still sail in summer from Norway to various parts of Britain. The vessel here is in dry dock in Shetland.

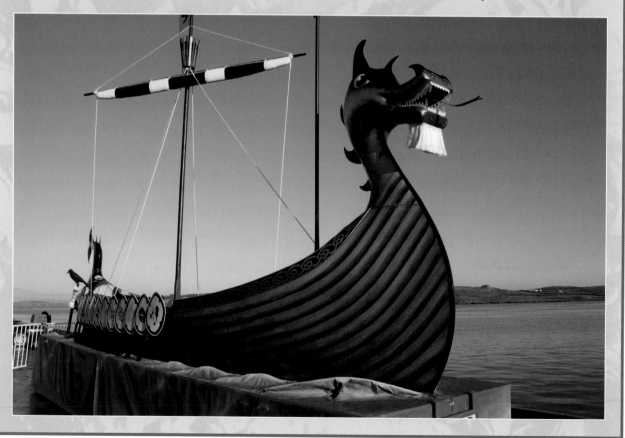

Black Sea and the Caspian Sea. In return for half of the proceeds, the Khazars agreed to allow the Vikings to sail up their rivers on the way to plunder Arab territories beyond the Caspian Sea. However, the Khazars underestimated the ferocity of the Viking raids.

When the Khazars heard how the Vikings had ravaged the countryside, burning towns and massacring the inhabitants, they assembled an army and confronted the Vikings on their return. In the ensuing battle, the Viking leader (probably Oleg) was killed.

Oleg's successor, Igor, was murdered in 945 CE by Derevlian Slavs (from whom he had demanded very high taxes), but his widow, Olga, proved to be a formidable ruler. Ruling at first as regent for her young son, Svyatoslav, she ruthlessly eliminated the Derevlian opposition. Even after Svyatoslav took over, Olga remained the power behind the throne for the next 24 years.

Svyatoslav wanted to extend his kingdom even farther. If he could conquer territory as far as the Volga River, he reasoned, he would then control all the trade routes between the Baltic Sea and the Caspian Sea. In the 960s CE, Svyatoslav marched his army to the Khazar capital of Itl, on the banks of the Volga River. He destroyed the city and then subdued much of the lower Danube region, thereby tripling the size of his dominions. However, during his long absence from Kiev, the city had been besieged by the Pechenegs, a warrior people from central Asia, so he was forced to hurry home to save his mother and his children.

This 10th-century-CE Viking amulet depicts the hammer used by the Norse god Thor to produce thunder.

Having forced the Pechenegs to withdraw, Svyatoslav appointed his three sons as regents and marched on Constantinople. However, a defeat in 971 CE forced him to make peace with the Byzantine Empire. On the return journey to Kiev in 972 CE, Svyatoslav and his men were ambushed by the Pechenegs and massacred.

Svyatoslav's son Vladimir was keen to maintain good relations with Constantinople. In 988 CE, the Byzantine emperor Basil II offered his sister Anna's hand in marriage to Vladimir—on condition that Vladimir convert to Christianity. Because Anna would bring lands in the Crimea as her dowry and the marriage would create an alliance with Constantinople, Vladimir accepted. His baptism was a momentous occasion in the history of Russia. In the years that followed, many of his subjects abandoned their old pagan gods and embraced the new faith. The spread of Orthodox Christianity in Russia meant that the country would forever be under the influence of the eastern church.

Iceland and beyond

From the eighth century CE, the Norwegian Vikings had used the Shetland Islands (between Norway and Scotland) as a convenient base from which to launch attacks on the coastal settlements of Britain. In the ninth century CE, Viking ships appeared near the Faroe Islands, 200 miles (320 km) north of the Shetlands, and before long, the islands were colonized by Vikings, driving out the Irish monks who had previously inhabited them.

In the middle of the ninth century CE, several Viking sailors were blown off course and finished up 600 miles (960 km) west of Norway, on a large and apparently uninhabited island. One of the seafarers, Raven Floki, spent the summer there, living on salmon and seal. The favorable weather conditions gave Floki and his companions a false sense of security; they were quite unprepared for the severity of the winter that followed, and when they managed to make it back to Norway, they gave the island its discouraging name—Iceland.

Despite that unpromising start, many other Vikings followed in Floki's footsteps and, better prepared than he had been, successfully settled the island. There was plenty of land suitable for farming, an abundance of fish, and vast forests to yield timber for building. Within 60 years, it is estimated that the population of Iceland exceeded 10,000.

In the late ninth century CE, a warrior named Harald Finehair (ruled 860–930 CE) overcame all his rivals and became the first king of Norway. The emergence of a monarchy prompted many Norwegians to abandon their homes and seek new lands in which they could live without having to obey a ruler they had never wanted.

By 930 CE, so many Norwegian settlers had arrived in Iceland that there was little workable land left for the taking. As even more and more colonists continued to pour in, quarrels arose, and it became necessary to form

The illustrations on this Viking ornamental stone, carved and inscribed around 800 CE, depict Valhalla and a typical longship.

This waterfall stands on Thingvellir, the plain on which the people of Iceland held their first national assembly.

some sort of government. A republic was set up, governed by a parliament known as the Althing, which met once a year at midsummer. Regional bodies, called Things, met more often, and every freeman was eligible to attend and speak at them. The Thing had great powers. It could make laws, act as a law court, and even make the decision to go to war.

Around the beginning of the 11 century CE, Iceland became Christianized. By that time, most European countries, including those of Scandinavia, were already Christian, and pressure was brought to bear on the Icelanders to conform. At a meeting of the Althing, it was decided to adopt Christianity as the community's official religion, although pagan practices were still allowed. The compromise seemed to satisfy everyone, and the whole population was baptized en masse.

Greenland

After 930 CE, when most of the best land in Iceland had been taken, Viking settlers started looking even farther afield. From the most westerly point of Iceland, it was sometimes possible to catch a glimpse of a coast to the west. At one point, a sailor named Gunnbjörn Ulfsson was swept past Iceland during a violent storm and made landfall on some unprepossessing rocks that became known as Gunnbjörn's Skerries. Ulfsson

WHO WERE THE VIKINGS?

The Vikings were descendants of Germanic tribes who migrated to northern Europe around 2000 BCE. They eventually settled in Scandinavia—present-day Norway, Sweden, and Denmark—where they became farmers and traders. They were a pagan people, worshipping the Nordic gods—whose king was Odin, the god of war and death. Another important god was Thor, the god of thunder and lightning. The Norse myths are powerful stories that were passed orally from generation to generation until the 12th century CE, when they were first written down by scribes in Iceland.

Most Vikings were freemen. They either tilled the land (growing crops such as grain, vegetables, and fruit and keeping animals such as goats, cattle, and sheep) or were craftsmen and merchants. Below these freemen were slaves, many of whom had been captured during raids. Slaves worked as laborers on the farms and manned the oars on the longships. They had a life of unremitting hardship, and they had no rights. At the top of society were the nobles and chieftains, each of whom might command the services of freemen in the numerous internal struggles for land or on pirate voyages to seize loot or land abroad.

The Vikings lived in villages of single-story wooden huts that had roofs of turf but no windows. At the center of some villages, there was a larger longhouse in which the chieftain lived with his family, farmworkers, and animals. The most powerful chieftains controlled very large regions. They often went to war with rival leaders to eliminate competition and increase their own landholdings.

and other Viking mariners soon became convinced that there was land even farther to the west.

The first Scandinavian to venture intentionally into the unknown waters off the west coast of Iceland was an Icelandic farmer named Erik the Red. His decision to travel was forced on him by his local Thing, which, in 982 CE, banished him for three years for murdering the son of one of his neighbors. With nowhere else to go, Erik fitted out a ship and embarked on a desperate journey in search of land that no one knew existed. After four days' sailing, he and his crew sighted a forbidding coastline of towering cliffs. Turning southward, they sailed on until they found a safe haven on the coast. They disembarked at the southern tip of what appeared to be a very large island. There were green meadows for crops and grazing, and Erik and his party

This cloisonné brooch, with precious gemstones inlaid in enamel, was made by Norwegian Vikings in the seventh century CE.

settled there for three years. During that time, they explored the territory, and although the northern part of it (which was above the Arctic Circle) was icy and uninhabitable, the southern part (which was warmed by the Gulf Stream) offered plenty of cultivatable land. At the end of his enforced exile, Erik the Red returned to Iceland with enthusiastic reports of this new region, ripe for the taking, which he optimistically named Greenland.

In 986 CE, Erik the Red led a fleet carrying settlers and their livestock in a sortie to set up a colony on Greenland. Of the 25 ships that set out, only 14 made landfall on Greenland; the others were lost in storms and ice floes along the way. Around 450 surviving members of the expedition set up a colony on the west coast, where the deep fjords reminded them of their native Norway. Although life was hard, the settlers prospered, and a Viking community remained in Greenland for almost 500 years.

The New World

Erik the Red's second son, Leif Eriksson (c. 970–1020 CE), inherited his father's adventurous spirit. As a boy, he had heard the tale of an Icelander named Bjarni Herjolfsson—who, having been blown off course while attempting to sail to Greenland, sighted an unexplored land far to the west. Refusing to make landfall on this strange coastline, which he noted was well forested, Bjarni turned and sailed east for four days before reaching his intended destination, the coast of Greenland.

Around 1000 CE, Eriksson bought Bjarni's ship and planned an expedition to discover and explore the unknown country. Setting sail from Greenland, Eriksson followed the course of Bjarni's homeward voyage and, after several days, made landfall at a place that is thought to have been Baffin Island in modern Canada. He named his discovery

This 20th-century-CE statue of Leif Eriksson is one of the great monuments in Reykjavik, Iceland.

Helluland (the land of flat stones). Continuing south, Eriksson found a densely wooded stretch of coastline, which he named Markland (forest land)— and which may have been Labrador. After two further days at sea, the expedition sighted land for a third time and decided to go ashore for the winter. The place, which Eriksson named Vinland, is now known as Newfoundland. There, in 1960 CE, archaeologists unearthed an extensive Viking settlement that may have been Eriksson's encampment. Now fully excavated, the site at L'Anse aux Meadows consists of turf houses (that would have accommodated around 90 people), a smithy, and facilities for repairing ships. It is possible that the Vikings explored even farther to the south.

Eriksson returned to Greenland and reported that he had found a fertile, well-endowed land. Three more Viking voyages were made to Vinland, but the settlers abandoned their attempts to establish a colony in the face of hostility from the indigenous Native Americans.

Although that episode ended Viking attempts to colonize North America, it may not have been the last time that Scandinavian adventurers visited the New World. It is thought that, for several centuries, mariners from Iceland and Greenland continued to sail westward in search of new sources of wood, a prized commodity that was in very short supply in their native lands. What is certain, however, is that Leif Eriksson reached the New World around 500 years before it was "discovered" by Christopher Columbus.

See also:

The Carolingian Empire (volume 6, page 804) • Feudal Europe (volume 6, page 814) • From Kiev to Moscow (volume 9, page 1208)

FROM KIEV TO MOSCOW

The earliest Russian civilization emerged around the sixth century CE. Its first great power base was Kiev, but the city gradually surrendered its preeminence to Moscow, which became the capital in the 16th century CE.

While the history of every state is critically affected by its geography, there is perhaps no country in which the landscape and topography have had as great an influence on human events as they have had in Russia. Russia's most striking characteristic is, of course, its great size, but also important has been its lack of natural land boundaries. In the south of the country, the enormous open steppes provided an easy invasion route for nomadic, mounted tribesmen from central Asia. Similarly, in the west, the absence of a clearly defined natural frontier encouraged incursions from inhabitants of the plains of Europe. The heart of Russia, however, was sharply defined by its principal rivers, especially the Dnieper, the Don, and the Volga, which all flow from north to south and offer great potential for trade. The story of medieval Russia may be divided into four phases: the creation of a state based on river-borne trading opportunities; the breakup of that state as trade declined and pressure from the steppe nomads became irresistible; the creation of a new state that was independent from those nomads; and that state dealing with threats from its western neighbors.

At some time before the fourth century CE, Slavic peoples migrated from the Caucasus to the vast plains between the Black Sea and the Arctic Ocean to settle the area that became known as Russia. The Slavs were mainly hunters and traders. They used the rivers in the region to transport goods between the Baltic Sea and the Black Sea. As commercial activity developed, trading posts were established along the rivers. One of those trading posts was Novgorod, on the Volkhov River, and another was Kiev (Kyiv) on the Dnieper River. By the middle of the sixth century CE, Kiev was firmly established as the most important city in the region. The early inhabitants of Russia had to deal with steppe peoples such as the Avars and, later, the Khazars, who founded a powerful empire based in the lower Volga region.

The first great Russian state was created by the Varangians (Scandinavian Vikings from the area that is now Sweden), who traded and raided deep into Russia along the rivers. The Varangians were ruled by princes, one of whom was named Rurik.

In the ninth century CE, Rurik established himself in Novgorod and united the tribes of northern Russia. Many historians regard Rurik as the founder of the Russian Empire, and it is

This mosaic of the Virgin Mary is located in Saint Sophia's Cathedral in Kiev, which was the site of the initial Russian conversion to Christianity.

This woodcut shows a 19th-century-CE artist's impression of Rurik, the ninth-century-CE warrior who united the peoples of northern Russia from his base in Novgorod.

Russian state, Kievan Rus. Around 907 CE, Oleg made a treaty with the Byzantine Empire that allowed Kievan Rus to control and profit from all the trade between the Baltic Sea and Constantinople.

Oleg died soon after signing that treaty. He was succeeded by Igor, who ruled for three decades and greatly expanded the empire. On Igor's death in 945 CE, the throne passed to his widow, Olga. Olga further extended Kievan influence. Meanwhile, a new external threat had emerged—the Pechenegs, a warlike, seminomadic people from the southern steppes.

In 964 CE, Olga's son, Svyatoslav, came of age and inherited the throne. By the time Svyatoslav was ambushed and killed by Pechenegs in 972 CE, he had developed his kingdom into a large empire that included much of modern Ukraine. After Svyatoslav's death, his three sons fought each other for the throne. Eventually, the youngest son, Vladimir, became the undisputed ruler of Kievan Rus.

Vladimir the Great

Vladimir the Great (Vladimir I; ruled 980–1015 CE) is widely regarded as the architect of the Kievan state. He consolidated his empire, which now extended from Ukraine to the Baltic Sea, and strengthened its borders so that his armies were better equipped to repel raids by the steppe nomads.

Vladimir was also responsible for converting the people of Kievan Rus to Orthodox Christianity. This decision was primarily political rather than spiritually motivated. Vladimir himself was a pagan; he was more interested in overcoming his enemies and in the pursuit of his own pleasures than in religious matters. However, in 988 CE, the Byzantine emperor Basil II, to express his gratitude for Kievan help in suppressing a rebel-

certain that he ushered in a period of expansion, during which the Slavic peoples migrated north, replacing or assimilating the indigenous populations.

Varangians led by Askold and Dir penetrated farther south along the Dnieper River, reaching Kiev and, finally, Constantinople, which they attacked in 860 CE. In 879 CE, Rurik was succeeded by his son, Igor. Igor was still a child, so Oleg was appointed regent. In 882 CE, Oleg had the rulers of Kiev (Askold and Dir) assassinated and made Kiev the capital of the first significant

POWER IN THE EMPIRE OF KIEV

The political history of Kiev begins with Oleg's conquest of the city in 882 CE. It is not clear, however, when the Kiev Empire ceased to exist. Some historians maintain that the end of the empire coincided with the death of Yaroslav the Wise in 1054 CE, while others assert that Vladimir Monomachus (ruled 1113–1125 CE) was the last ruler. Alternatively, the last Kievan emperor may have been Mstislav (ruled 1125–1132 CE). A few historians see the conquest of Kiev by Andrew Bogolyubsky in 1169 CE as the end of the empire. The most convenient date is probably 1240 CE, when Kiev was destroyed by the Mongols.

The most important political institutions in Kievan Rus were the office of prince, the duma (council of boyars), and the *veche* (city council). The prince of Kiev held a very special position. From the early 12th century CE, he was called the grand prince. He commanded the army, controlled the administration of justice, and was the head of government. In times of war, the grand prince called first on his *druzhina* (his personal liegemen). In extreme cases, he could order a general mobilization of all his subjects.

Kievan Rus was very well organized, especially where trade and finance were concerned, and the penalties that were imposed by the legal system tended to be fines rather than physical punishments. The government raised finances by taxing fireplaces and plowshares and by levying duties on trade.

The duma worked in consultation with the grand prince but could not overrule him. The *veche*, however, which convened in the marketplace, had much greater powers. Its decisions in emergencies and in conflicts between members of the ruling families appear to have been highly influential and often binding. The effectiveness of the Kievan *veche* inspired the creation of similar bodies in other Russian cities, notably Novgorod, which had its own *veche* until it was taken over by Moscow.

This watercolor by Russian artist Victor Vasnetsov (1848–1926 CE) depicts Oleg, who seized power in Kiev in the ninth century CE.

The fourth longest river in Europe, the Dnieper flows for 1,367 miles (2,200 km) from its source near Moscow to the Black Sea. This photograph shows a stretch of the river near its estuary outside Kiev.

lion, offered his sister Anna's hand in marriage to Vladimir. A condition of the marriage was that Vladimir should convert to his bride's religion, Orthodox Christianity. Because Anna's dowry included rich and extensive Byzantine lands, Vladimir was happy to agree.

Once Vladimir had been baptized, he made Orthodox Christianity the official religion of Kievan Rus. From that time onward, the Orthodox Church played a major role in the development of Russian society. One lasting consequence of the conversion was the adoption in Russia of the Cyrillic alphabet, which was very different from the Roman alphabet used in most of Europe.

On the death of Vladimir in 1015 CE, the throne was seized by his eldest son, Svyatopolk the Accursed, who lost no time in killing two of his brothers. Another brother, Yaroslav, the regent of Novgorod, then enlisted the aid of Scandinavian mercenaries to depose Svyatopolk in 1019 CE.

By 1036 CE, Yaroslav had created a great Russian empire that stretched from the Black Sea to the Gulf of Finland. Unlike most of his predecessors, Yaroslav was interested in art and culture. He collected manuscripts of all kinds, and he commissioned scholars to translate Greek texts into Russian. He also built churches and monasteries and started to codify the law, an initiative that formed the basis of the legal code known as Russian Justice.

Yaroslav tried to establish a system of inheritance to avoid the internecine struggles that had been the norm following the deaths of previous grand princes of Kiev. However, his efforts were to no avail. After his own death in 1054 CE, most of Vladimir's numerous grandsons inherited lands and acquired interests in conflict with each other. A profusion of warring city-states developed, most of

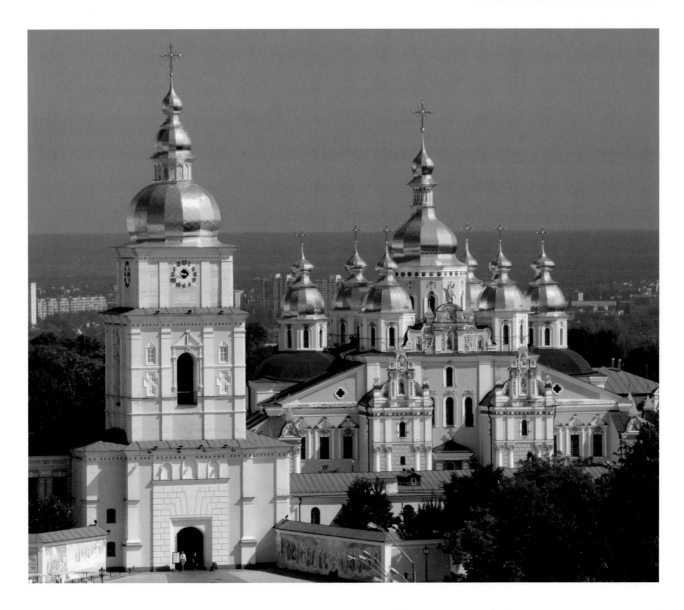

them ruled by vying members of the royal house of Rurik.

The decline of Kiev

During the second half of the 11th century CE, disputes between the competing city-states became more acrimonious and increasingly involved the nomadic peoples in the south of the country. The conflicts weakened Kievan Rus, which lost much of its former cohesion and was sometimes in danger of disintegrating. Yaroslav's grandson, Vladimir Monomachus (ruled 1113–1125 CE), tried to restore order, but his efforts were never fully successful.

An important factor in Kiev's decline was the increasingly difficult trading conditions. Kiev was badly affected when soldiers of the Fourth Crusade sacked Constantinople in 1204 CE. Many citizens of Kiev left for Novgorod, which was increasingly looking west to the Baltic Sea for trade; indeed, in the 13th century CE, the Hanseatic League of German cities used Novgorod as its base in Russia. Important western regions of the Kievan state, such as Galicia and Volhynia, established independent links with Hungary and Poland, while central authority was also challenged by the boyars (landed nobility).

Built in the 18th century CE, Saint Michael's Monastery, with its distinctive golden domes, overlooks the city of Kiev.

The walls of the kremlin (citadel) in Novgorod overlook the Volkhov River.

It was in this severely weakened condition that the Kievan state was forced to face a new adversary that threatened its very existence.

The Mongols

The new threat to Kiev came from the Mongol army of Genghis Khan (1162–1227 CE), which marauded westward from central Asia. The first Mongol incursion into Russia came from the Caucasus and was led by two sons of Genghis. The Mongols later reached the Crimea, and at the mouth of the Dnieper River, they defeated an alliance of Kievan forces and the Polovtsi (a local steppe people). After their victory, the Mongols were recalled to take part in an invasion of China. In 1237 CE, however, they returned. Batu Khan, grandson of Genghis, led Mongol forces in an invasion that destroyed the major Russian cities in the Vladimir-Suzdal region. Batu Khan sacked Kiev in 1240 CE, and Alexander Nevsky saved the city of Novgorod only by the payment of a substantial ransom.

The Mongols then rode westward again, defeating Christian armies in Germany and Hungary. Their advance was halted in 1241 CE, when they learned of the death of Genghis Khan's heir, Ogotai. On hearing the news, they returned, as they were bound to do under their laws, to Mongolia to settle the succession.

For the next 200 years, Russian political life was dominated by the authority of the Mongol state in the steppes. Effectively, southern Russia became part of what was called the Empire of the Golden Horde. The Mongols made their capital at Sarai, and it was to that city on the lower Volga River that all the Russian principalities had to send tributes to the khans of the Golden Horde. In Sarai, the Russian principalities were represented by the grand prince of Russia, who had to travel to the city to perform obeisance to a representative of the Golden Horde. In addition, Russian military contingents were occasionally required to serve in Mongol forces.

In 1380 CE, the Russians scored a significant victory over the Mongols when Dmitry Donskoy, the grand duke of Moscow, defeated the forces of the Golden Horde at the Battle of Kulikovo on the Don River. However, a resurgent Golden Horde counterattacked and captured Moscow in 1382 CE.

Moscow and Novgorod

Although the khans of the Golden Horde demanded tribute and obeisance, they did not interfere in the day-to-day activities of the Russian principalities. Novgorod, for example, thrived as a trading city. It developed its own unique governing system, based on the rule of several important trading families, tempered by the importance of the division of the town into "fifths" and the existence of a *veche* (town council). Other important centers included the cities of Pskov and Tver.

However, it was Moscow that gradually became both the heart and the strongest arm of the new Russian state. The first of the great dukes of Moscow was Daniel Nevsky, who inherited the town from his father, Alexander Nevsky, in 1263 CE. Daniel Nevsky established a dynasty in Moscow that eventually became the sovereign power of Russia. Daniel's son, Ivan I, took over in 1328 CE and was permitted by the Mongols to annex territory to Moscow.

Moscow was just one of several almost equally important Russian principalities until the rule of Vasily II, who came to the throne as a 10-year-old in 1425 CE. Vasily used alliances with Lithuania and within the Golden Horde to secure the supremacy of his city.

Moscow's rulers used the fall of Constantinople to the Ottoman Turks in 1453 CE to strengthen their position further. Moscow became regarded by the Russian church and princes as "the third Rome," the true heir to the Byzantine Empire. In 1473 CE, Ivan III, who was grand prince of Moscow from 1462 to 1505 CE, married a niece of the last Byzantine emperor. From 1474 CE, Ivan called himself czar (Slavic for "caesar" or

This 16th-century-CE manuscript illustration depicts the siege of Kozelsk in 1238 CE. Kozelsk was one of many Russian cities attacked by Mongol forces under Batu Khan.

LITHUANIA, POLAND, AND HUNGARY

Russia's history during the medieval period was closely entwined with that of three states to its west—Hungary, Poland, and Lithuania. The borders among all four of them ebbed and flowed as power shifted in the region. Hungary, for example, became dominant in western parts of the Kievan realm during the latter's decline in the 12th century CE, while the rivalry between Russia and Poland was not finally settled until the latter was partitioned in the 18th century CE.

All four states suffered severely during the Mongol domination of the southern European steppes, and they all fought against the Teutonic Knights at various times in the 14th and 15th centuries CE. For a while, Poland was united with Hungary, but from 1386 CE, Poland and Lithuania were brought together to form the largest state in Europe under the ruling Jagiellon dynasty.

Poland and Hungary converted to Catholicism early in the Middle Ages, and as a result, their cultural development was quite different from that of Orthodox Russia. Lithuania was a pagan culture until 1386 CE, when the grand duke converted to Catholicism in order to become king of Poland (Wladyslaw II).

Hungary was a major power in the 14th and 15th centuries CE. Under King Matthias Corvinus (ruled 1458–1490 CE), the nation fought successful campaigns against the Ottoman Turks, who were encroaching north from the Balkan Peninsula, and against the Holy Roman emperor Frederick III. In 1485 CE, Corvinus took Vienna and annexed large areas of what is now Austria. The power politics of eastern Europe during this period were complex. Russian rulers frequently allied with the Ottomans and the steppe nomads against the Catholic states of Poland and Hungary.

This oil painting by 20th-century-CE Russian artist Alexander Bubnov depicts the Battle of Kulikovo in 1380 CE.

"emperor"). He annexed Novgorod in 1478 CE and Tver in 1485 CE. Also in 1485 CE, the Russian princes stopped paying tribute to the Mongols.

Threat from the west

Ivan III's successes against the Golden Horde were in stark contrast to the failure of his policies toward the Swedes and the Polish-Lithuanian state. The Russian borders with those realms had no natural frontiers, and any state or organization that had an army and wanted to extend its territory could do so almost with impunity. For example, during the later period of the Kievan state, Russian princes from Novgorod raided what is now Estonia on many occasions. From the early 13th century CE, the Teutonic Knights of Livonia (formed in 1237 CE from a previous crusading order, the Swordbrothers) became a major power on the Baltic coast. Alexander Nevsky defeated them at the Battle of Lake Peipus in 1242 CE, but the knights remained a threat until the Lithuanians defeated them at the Battle of Tannenberg (also known as the Battle of Grunwald) in 1410 CE. Lithuania then confronted Russia. Ivan III encouraged attacks against Poland-Lithuania by former subjects of the Golden Horde (such as the Crimean Tartars), but his long wars in the late 15th century CE were inconclusive. Similarly, Ivan fought a series of wars against the Swedes who ruled in Finland, but again, there was no decisive success.

Ivan III was succeeded by Vasily III (ruled 1505–1533 CE), who completed the absorption of the old Russian principalities by Moscow, taking control of Pskov in 1510 CE and Ryazan in 1521 CE. There was now a Russian state, with Moscow as its capital, that had a clear unity of culture and language. The birth of modern Russia is normally agreed to coincide with the accession of Ivan IV (ruled 1533–1584 CE), known as Ivan the Terrible, who introduced an effective central administration and created an empire that incorporated non-Slav states. It is for that reason that Ivan the Terrible is known as the first "Czar of All the Russias."

See also:

The Mongols (volume 9, page 1218) • The Vikings (volume 9, page 1196)

This 16th-century-CE engraving depicts Ivan III, the first grand prince of Moscow to take the title czar.

THE MONGOLS

Between the 13th and 15th centuries CE, the Mongols created the largest land empire that the world has ever seen. At the height of their power, the Mongols ruled the greater part of Asia, as well as central Europe up to the eastern frontier of Germany.

The Mongols were nomadic herders from a predominantly grassland area that surrounds the Gobi Desert in eastern Asia and is bordered by mountains to the east and the west.

During the 13th and 14th centuries CE, Mongol armies rode out of their heartland to conquer vast expanses of Asia, the Middle East, and Europe. They created the largest land empire the world has ever seen, stretching from the Pacific Ocean to the Black Sea and including most of China. They might have conquered Europe and the Middle East but for their custom of suspending their campaigns every time one of their khans (emperors) died.

Genghis Khan

The roots of Mongol expansionism can be traced to around 1162 CE, when Yesukai, a Mongol chieftain living near Lake Baikal, fathered a child named Temujin. Yesukai led a loose alliance of around 30,000 families who sometimes went to war against rival nomads but whose principal activities were sheep farming and hunting.

At age 13, Temujin inherited his father's role as tribal chief, but his succession was not unopposed; he was forced into hiding, and on several occasions, he was almost killed by rivals. However, Temujin gave an early demonstration of his skill as a politician and his ferocity as a warrior by overcoming all his adversaries. By 1190 CE, his leadership was acknowledged throughout the greater part of Mongolia.

In 1206 CE, Temujin convened a *kurultai* (gathering of tribal leaders), which he reputedly addressed with these words: "Those who share my fortune, and whose loyalty is as clear as glass, may call themselves Mongols and their power shall be above everything that lives."

Temujin went on to declare the assembly of families, clans, and tribes to be a single nation, and he offered them dominion over the whole world. The gathering then proclaimed him ruler of all the Mongols and conferred on him the title Genghis Khan. *Genghis* is derived from the Chinese for "valued warrior"; *Khan* comes from the Turkish for "lord."

From his capital in Karakorum, Genghis Khan announced a simple manifesto—there could be only one ruler and all opponents would be put to death. He decreed that his successors as khan must be elected, in perpetuity, by the *kurultai*. That stipulation had ultimately fatal consequences for the Mongols.

This medieval manuscript illustration depicts Genghis Khan and his mounted warriors in one of their battles.

وبوضعی که نام آن بیده ی قورقانت با جاموقه مصاف داد واورابشکست وقوم قنقرات ما

THE MONGOL EMPIRE

KEY

▨ Mongol lands around 1206 CE

▦ Lands gained between 1206 and 1227 CE

▨ Lands gained between 1227 and 1259 CE

✕ Major battle

Genghis Khan also demanded that no Mongol leader could make peace with an opponent unless that opponent had first acknowledged the authority of the khan. The khan himself acknowledged only the authority of the Great Yasa, a code created by Genghis Khan himself.

The Great Yasa was based on the laws of a Turkic people, the Uighurs, and included some rules that were new to the Mongols but that were of great use to them during the conquests on which they were about to embark. For example, the code permitted Mongols to drink the blood and eat the entrails of animals, practices that had traditionally been forbidden. During the great Mongol expeditions, the blood of horses became an important source of food for the cavalrymen.

Also codified in the Great Yasa was the division of labor between husband and wife. The husband was to hunt and fight, while the wife was to take care of business and the family property.

Every Mongol had equal rights under the Great Yasa. No Mongol was to enslave or fight another Mongol. Horse stealing and adultery, which were regarded as the most serious crimes, were punishable by death. The usual penalty for lesser crimes was flogging. Mongols were not required to pay taxes.

Genghis Khan was a brilliant military commander and strategist. His army was renowned for its organization and discipline. His archers (who used composite bows made of horn and wood glued together) became famous for their accuracy and rapid shooting. At the lowest level, the army was divided into units of 10 men, who were obliged to stay together under all circumstances. There was one commander for every 100 men (10 units). Above the commanders were senior officers in charge of every 1,000 soldiers. The largest unit, known as a *touman*, comprised 10,000 soldiers and was commanded by an *orkon*, a deputy of the khan.

The Mongols were superb horsemen, and each soldier took at least two or three horses with him on every campaign. The khan's greatest concern was to have sufficient horses for his military requirements. He would often delay attacks for years while he waited to assemble the right number.

During campaigns, the Mongols lived off the land and ate whatever they could

scavenge. Most of their horses were mares, and the mares' milk provided a large part of their diet, but on long marches through barren steppes, the men would drink the blood of their horses. Three things about the Mongols particularly amazed their enemies: their endurance, their mobility, and their extreme cruelty to the vanquished.

It is said that Genghis Khan once asked one of his captains what he considered the greatest pleasure for a man. The captain replied, "Hunting with his people in the steppes on a beautiful day with his horse at the gallop."

"No," said the khan. "The greatest pleasure for a warrior is to trample his foe under foot, to seize his horse and riches, and to hear the wailing of inconsolable women." The great khan and his successors certainly embodied that atti-

Landscape such as this is typical of central Mongolia. Under Genghis Khan, the indigenous people rode out from this heartland to subjugate the greater part of Eurasia.

This 20th-century-CE French engraving depicts Genghis Khan (center) taking advice from Chinese fortune-tellers.

the Chinese emissaries with scorn. "Let your emperor know that it is a matter of indifference to us whether he regards us as a friend or a foe," Genghis Khan told them. "If he wants to be our friend, then we will let him rule his territory under our authority, but if he would rather have war, then we will fight until one of us is totally destroyed."

After the delegation had departed, the Mongols prepared for war. They collected enormous numbers of horses and made millions of arrows. Around 1200 CE, a well-equipped cavalry army crossed the Great Wall of China. The following years were disastrous for northern China. By 1208 CE, the Mongols were well established in China, although they had difficulty in taking some Chinese cities, because the cities were fortified with towers and walls. The invaders withdrew to the Mongolian steppes every winter and returned the following summer to continue the invasion.

One of Genghis Khan's greatest attributes was his ability to recognize expertise or knowledge that the Mongols did not have. In the same way that he had previously adapted a Turkic legal code, he now hired Chinese generals to teach the Mongols about the technology and tactics of siege warfare. He also employed Chinese bureaucrats who could read and write (most Mongols were illiterate) and knew how to organize the government of a settled society, particularly the collection of taxes.

In 1213 CE, Genghis Khan led his army into the Shandong Peninsula. Within a year, he had conquered the Manchus, who were themselves of Mongolian descent. He took Yenking (modern Beijing) in 1215 CE, razing most of the city to the ground and installing one of his *orkons* as the city's administrator.

In 1217 CE, Genghis Khan turned his attention to the west. His new target

tude. Hulagu, grandson of Genghis Khan, boasted in a letter to Louis IX of France that he was personally responsible for 200,000 deaths in his raids into lands that are now part of Iran, Iraq, and Syria.

Genghis Khan's first campaign was against northern China, where the Western Xia people had established their own state. The Western Xia assumed that Genghis Khan would continue to pay tribute to them as his father had always done.

When a new Xia emperor, Wai Wang, was crowned, his ministers sent a delegation to Genghis Khan to demand a renewed oath of fealty. The khan treated was the powerful Khoresm Empire, based in central Asia and Persia. When the khan was told that the Khoresm Muslims would be more powerful than the Chinese, he assembled his hordes and issued the following warning: "It is necessary for a leader of 10 men to be as alert and obedient as the leader of 10,000 men. Anyone who fails in this shall die, together with his wife and children."

The campaigns against the Khoresm emperor Mohammed Shah were remarkable for the speed of Mongol advance and for the khan's bold strategic moves. Cities that surrendered at once, such as Bukhara, were spared, but cities that resisted, such as Samarkand, were sacked and the populations were massacred. During this period, Mongol forces turned south into the Indian Subcontinent to take Peshawar and Lahore. By 1221 CE, the Mongols held sway throughout central Asia and much of Persia.

Another Mongol army then moved through the Caucasus to the mouth of the Dnieper River and crushed a Russian force at the Battle of the Kalka River (near Donetsk, a city in modern Ukraine) in 1223 CE before returning to central Asia.

In 1224 CE, Genghis Khan launched a new campaign in China to break up an anti-Mongol alliance between the Xia and Jin empires. By the time Genghis Khan died in August of 1227 CE, the Mongol Empire covered much of Asia, from the steppes of what is now southern Russia to the China Sea.

Genghis Khan was succeeded by his son Ogotai, who continued the extension of Mongol power, particularly in China. Ogotai was followed by Kuguk and then by Mangu. Mangu was suc-

This 14th-century-CE Persian miniature depicts Mongol yurts.

This 15th-century-CE drawing on vellum depicts a Mongolian nomad, in traditional attire, taking his horse to water.

ceeded by his brother Kublai Khan (ruled 1260–1294 CE).

Kublai Khan

Kublai Khan, a grandson of Genghis Khan, took the Mongol Empire to the height of its power, controlling much of the Eurasian land mass. Before his election as great khan in 1260 CE, Kublai Khan spent seven years with Mangu attempting to complete their grandfather's conquest of China. They fought the Song dynasty in the south and stamped out all resistance in the north.

Although, in theory, Kublai Khan was overlord of the whole Mongol Empire, his principal khanate was China. He established his capital at Khan-balik (modern Cambaluc, near Beijing), where his court became internationally famous. The Venetian merchant-adventurer Marco Polo visited the court, and his

memoirs provide insights into the Mongol Empire of the period.

To administer China, the new khan employed a host of talented Chinese and Muslim officials. He adopted the Chinese bureaucratic system but excluded Chinese people from positions of power. The previous Mongol way of life—with its unquestioning obedience to military leaders, reliance on a nomadic lifestyle, and scorn for farmers—did not fit easily into the sophisticated, urban civilization of China. As the caravan routes across central Asia became safe under Mongol control, many more traders and missionaries started to use them. The travelers encouraged increased intercultural contact and understanding but weakened the specifically Mongol way of life.

Kublai Khan's crowning achievement was the unification of China, which he

MARCO POLO

Marco Polo was born in Venice around 1254 CE. He was the son of Niccolò Polo, a prosperous merchant whose wealth was based on trade with Asia. At the age of 17, Marco Polo accompanied his father and his uncle, Maffeo, on a journey to the court of Kublai Khan in China. Once they finally arrived there, they remained for 17 years. During that time, Marco Polo was often employed by the emperor to travel around China on fact-finding missions, and his written accounts of these journeys have provided much information about the reign of Kublai Khan.

Around 1295 CE, the Polos finally returned to Venice, where they had long been presumed dead. Soon afterward, Marco Polo was captured by the Genoese in a sea battle and put in prison in Genoa. It was there that he dictated his book, *Il Milione* (The Million), which was an account (probably much embellished) of his travels through distant lands. Marco Polo was later freed from jail and returned to Venice, where he died in 1324 CE.

There are around 140 manuscript versions of *Il Milione*, and no two have identical text. It is often difficult to sort fact from fantasy, and it is almost impossible to tell which parts Marco Polo himself believed and which were merely reports of popular legends. The most skeptical historians have even doubted whether he went to China at all. Why, for example, does *Il Milione* make no reference to the Great Wall?

One story in *Il Milione* concerns Prester John, the mythical ruler of a Christian kingdom somewhere in the East. According to Marco Polo's account, Genghis Khan asked to marry Prester John's daughter, but the emissaries were arrogantly dismissed with these words: "How does Genghis Khan presume to ask for my daughter's hand when he knows he is only a servant of mine! Leave instantly and never return."

In this illustration from a 15th-century-CE edition of **Il Milione,** *Marco Polo is depicted purchasing goods from Chinese traders.*

This 13th-century-CE painting from China depicts Kublai Khan.

completed in 1279 CE through the subjugation of the Song dynasty. Then, Kublai Khan established the Yuan dynasty and became its first emperor.

Kublai Khan then made determined assaults on southeast Asia and forced the kings of Burma, Cambodia, and Annam (the northern part of modern Vietnam) to swear allegiance to him and give him tributes. He sent fleets to Java and Japan but failed to conquer them. Although the Mongol Empire reached its greatest extent under Kublai Khan, the protracted wars were a severe drain on China's (and therefore the Mongols') resources.

Kublai Khan was a Buddhist and made Buddhism the state religion in China, but adherents of other religions remained free to practice them. The emperor encouraged literature and the arts. During his reign, many extravagant buildings were constructed, and the Grand Canal was repaired and extended. Nevertheless, Mongol rule was always resented in China. Chinese officials objected to their reduced status, and the peasants struggled under heavy taxation. Kublai Khan died in 1294 CE, and by the 1340s CE, a combination of crop failures, famine, inflation, and catastrophic floods had led to widespread civil unrest. By the 1360s CE, a former

KUBLAI KHAN'S PALACE

While he was in China, Marco Polo lived at the court of Kublai Khan, and his book, *Il Milione*, gives a vivid description of the emperor's palace.

According to one passage: "It is larger than any I have ever seen. The roof—which is adorned with bronze and copper—is very lofty, and the sides of the great halls and apartments are ornamented with gold and silver. There are beautiful representations of warriors, women, birds, and beasts."

He goes on: "The grand hall is extremely long and permits dinners to be served to 6,000 people. The palace contains a large number of chambers. The exterior of the roof is adorned with a variety of colors and is painted so well that it shines like gold. The palace grounds are ornamented with many handsome trees and meadows in which are kept various kinds of beasts, such as stags, roebuck, and ermine. In the middle, there is a large lake containing all kinds of fish."

Buddhist monk named Zhu Yuanzhang had gained control of the Yangtze River Valley. In 1371 CE, the Mongols fled back to the steppes.

The Golden Horde

The territory that Genghis Khan had wanted to bequeath to his eldest son, Jochi, included all the lands west of the Aral Sea—the open steppes extending from Asia into Europe. However, Jochi predeceased his father, and Jochi's khanate became the realm of his own son, Batu Khan. Because of the magnificence of Batu Khan's camp, this part of the empire became known as the Golden Horde.

Batu Khan was determined to extend his territory. In 1237 CE, he crossed the Ural River to pillage the cities of the Vladimir-Suzdal region in central Russia.

In 1240 CE, his armies sacked Kiev and slaughtered its inhabitants. They then went on to Poland and Silesia, where they razed Lublin and Krakow. In 1241 CE, two Mongol columns advanced even farther westward. One column defeated an army of European knights at Liegnitz, west of the Oder River, on April 9. The other column crushed the forces of Bela IV, the Arpad king of Hungary, at the Sajo River on April 11. The Mongols then took the cities of Pest (part of modern Budapest) and Ragusa (modern Dubrovnik, Croatia). The Mongols were preparing an invasion of central Europe when news reached them in December of 1241 CE that Ogotai had died. Still abiding by the laws of Genghis Khan, they immediately withdrew to Mongolia to help settle the succession.

Created around 1630 CE, this copper engraving depicts the Battle of Liegnitz (1241 CE), in which the Mongols defeated an army of European knights.

1227

Tamerlane's capital, Samarkand, is one of the most important cities in modern Uzbekistan.

Although thwarted in its assault on central Europe, the Golden Horde established by Batu Khan extended the khanate from the Ural Mountains to the Carpathians, and from the Black Sea in the south to Siberia in the northeast. The Golden Horde flourished until the end of the 15th century CE, when it broke up into the separate khanates of Crimea, Sibir, Kazan, and Astrakhan. Not until 1485 CE did the Russian princes cease paying tribute to the Mongol capital of Sarai on the Volga River.

The Il-Khanate

The Il-Khanate, based in Persia (modern Iran), was established in 1256 CE by Hulagu, who was given instructions, after Mangu's accession, to extend Mongol power into Islamic regions. Hulagu led his horde through Persia, Mesopotamia, Armenia, and Georgia. In 1258 CE, Hulagu and his army stormed the Abbasid capital of Baghdad. They razed it to the ground and, according to some accounts, killed more than 800,000 people.

Hulagu then took Aleppo and Damascus. In 1260 CE, however, he was recalled to Karakorum because of the death of Mangu. Once again, the death of a great khan brought an end to a Mongol offensive.

The Mamluk rulers of Egypt took advantage of Hulagu's absence and, at the Battle of Ain Jalut in 1260 CE, defeated the small Mongol army that had been left behind in Syria. On his arrival at Karakorum, Hulagu discovered that his brother, Kublai Khan, had been campaigning successfully in China. The *kurultai* chose Kublai Khan to replace Mangu. Rebuffed, Hulagu returned to Persia, barely acknowledging the authority of his brother.

In a major example of the forces dragging the greater Mongol Empire apart, there was a short period of hostilities between the Il-Khanate and the Golden Horde. When Ghazan Khan came to power in 1295 CE, he refused outright to acknowledge the great khan. Ghazan Khan converted to Islam, and the traditional culture of Persia gradually became dominant at court. The power of the Il-Khanate weakened over the years, and when Khan Abu Said died without an heir in 1395 CE, native Persian rule was restored in a number of the small successor states that sprang up.

Tamerlane

In central Asia, Turkic tribes had been dominant until the Mongol conquest. Genghis Khan originally allotted this part of his realm—which roughly corresponds to modern Turkestan—to Jagatai, his second son.

After the death of Kublai Khan in 1294 CE, the Turkic peoples began asserting their independence from Mongol authority. The most important Turkic leader was Tamerlane (who was also of Mongol descent). Born in 1336 CE, he was nicknamed Timur the Lame because of a crippled leg. He became chief minister to the khan of the Jagatai Mongol realm and then took supreme power for himself around 1369 CE.

Tamerlane, a Muslim, made his capital at Samarkand and then set about enlarging his empire by force of arms. His ambition was to recreate the Mongol Empire as it had been under Genghis Khan. By 1394 CE, Tamerlane had conquered western Persia, Mesopotamia, Armenia, and Georgia. He first allied himself with, and then fought against, the Golden Horde, which never recovered

from his ruthless attacks. Tamerlane invaded India in 1398 CE, seizing Delhi and massacring its inhabitants. Moving westward, he attacked Syria in 1400 CE and slaughtered the inhabitants of Baghdad in 1401 CE. Tamerlane then invaded Anatolia (modern Turkey), defeating the Ottoman Turks and taking their capital, Ankara, in 1402 CE.

Tamerlane died in 1405 CE. In 1526 CE, one of his descendants, Babur, founded the Mughal dynasty in India.

This manuscript illustration, produced in Persia in 1533 CE, depicts the coronation of Tamerlane in Kabul after his conquest of Afghanistan en route from Baghdad to India.

See also:

From Kiev to Moscow (volume 9, page 1208)
• Turkish Empires and the Islamic World (volume 9, page 1230)

TURKISH EMPIRES AND THE ISLAMIC WORLD

Between 1000 and 1500 CE, a number of great Islamic states arose in the Mediterranean region. They included the Seljuk and Mamluk empires. These states often found themselves in conflict with another great regional power—the Mongols.

As the Abbasid caliphate declined in power from the mid-ninth century CE onward, power in the Islamic world became divided between a number of centers and a number of different groups of peoples. In spite of the decline of central power, and in spite of extremely destructive attacks on Islamic societies by peoples such as the Mongols, Islam continued to spread as a successful religion. The result was that by the year 1500 CE, the Islamic world was far larger than it had been in 1000 CE and threatened to surround the Christian states of Europe.

Common themes

There were certain important threads running through the Islamic world during the Middle Ages. One was the importance of trade (over both land and sea) in creating rich, prosperous cities that could recover from violent attacks. Islam's reach extended across the Indian Ocean to what is now Indonesia and was well established in the islands of Java and Sumatra by 1500 CE. Islamic traders were also spreading their religion and asserting political control along the coast of eastern Africa.

A second thread was the importance of missionaries in spreading Islam. The most influential missionaries were the Sufis (see box, page 1233), members of an Islamic sect that sought direct contact

with God. One way of getting into close contact with God was through dance, a practice that has come down to the modern day in the performances of the whirling dervishes. Although Sufis were often distrusted by political leaders within the Islamic world, their piety and asceticism were influential in encouraging conversion to Islam.

Another important thread was the practice of creating armed forces from groups of children who were removed from their families and brought up in closed military societies. Effectively, they were slaves, owing allegiance only to their political masters. Such societies could be extremely effective militarily: the Egyptian-based Mamluks defeated the previously all-conquering Mongols, for example, while the Janissaries who served the Ottoman rulers were also very successful. However, these societies could also turn on their masters, as the Mamluks did in Egypt.

Perhaps the most important factor in the continuing expansion of the Islamic world was the attraction that the religion had for many of the groups of people who might otherwise have been its enemies. An example were the Turkic tribes

This carpet was made by Mamluk textile workers. The Mamluks ruled Egypt between 1250 and 1517 CE.

This silver basin was made by Ayyubid craftsmen around 1240 CE.

of central Asia. Their fierce and strong nomadic culture made them a threat to the settled societies around them, but most of them had converted to Islam by 1000 CE. One of the first great states to be established by Turkic tribes was the Ghaznavid Empire. Its founder, Mahmud (ruled 998–1030 CE), took over large parts of Afghanistan, eastern Persia, and northwestern India. In Persia, the Ghaznavids were in turn defeated by another wave of Turkic invaders, the Ghuzz Turks. The Ghaznavids abandoned their Persian lands but flourished in northern India. The Ghaznavids were militantly Muslim and destroyed Hindu temples. They were the first of the great Muslim dynasties of India, and they were succeeded by further Muslim states, such as the Ghurid dynasty, the Delhi Sultanate, and finally the Mughal Empire, established by Babur in 1526 CE.

The rise of the Seljuks

One Ghuzz Turk clan was particularly successful after moving into the Ghaznavid territories of Persia: the Seljuks. After forcing the Ghaznavids to relinquish control of Persia, the Seljuks took Baghdad. In 1055 CE, they drove out the Shi'ite Buyids, who had asserted

effective control of the caliphate. Two energetic Seljuk rulers then created a vast empire. Alp Arslan (ruled 1063–1072 CE) conquered Syria and then inflicted a heavy defeat on the Christian forces of the Byzantine Empire at Manzikert in 1071 CE. Anatolia, the heart of the Byzantine Empire, now lay open to the Seljuks. Although Alp Arslan was killed fighting against the Qarakhanids (another Turkic people) in 1072 CE, his successor, Malik Shah (ruled 1072–1092 CE) occupied Anatolia and took over Palestine. On Malik Shah's death, the Seljuk Empire stretched from the Aegean Sea through most of what is now Iraq and Iran and on to lands east of the Aral Sea. It had failed to subdue the other major Islamic state in the Middle East (the Fatimids of Egypt) but was otherwise unchallenged.

This Seljuk state was difficult to maintain as a single entity, however. The range of cultures that it contained—from the sophisticated urban centers of Isfahan and Baghdad to the nomadic tribes of central Asia—had little in common, and the Seljuks were very reliant on Turkic tribesmen who were fiercely independent and mistrustful of any central authority. On Malik Shah's death, two

SUFIS AND SUFISM

Sufis were Muslim mystics who played an important role in the spread of Islam. The term *Sufi* probably derives from the Arabic word for "wool," a reference to the harsh woolen robes worn by certain early Muslim thinkers. Sufis were also know as "poor men"—*fakir* in Arabic and *dervish* in Persian. Both of these words have come into use in English.

Sufism grew out of a desire for a direct connection with God. Meditation on the Koran was an early way of making this connection, but Sufism quickly became associated with mystical poetry. Sufism tended initially to be passed through small groups, but in the 13th century CE, when the Mongol invasions posed a great threat to the Islamic world, Sufi brotherhoods were created.

In Sufi orders and brotherhoods, disciples swore allegiance to "masters" and often lived in the equivalent of monasteries. They undertook missionary activity around the borders of the Muslim world, particularly in central Asia, Africa, and India.

With their commitment to poverty and their strict discipline, Sufis were always an admired religious group, but their importance in the spread of Islam lay in how they expressed feelings during rituals and formal rites of passage such as marriages or funerals. Dancing, singing, and playing music created an atmosphere that was far removed from the often dry procedures of the more academic Islamic religious figures; the activities made Islam a more approachable religion.

However, the emotional and mystical aspects of Sufism also laid it open to criticism from more conventional Islamic thinkers. Sufis were always at pains to emphasize that they were in complete accord with shari'ah law and were not trying to undercut or ignore it. However, their mysticism often suggested a feeling that all of creation was one, and this almost pantheistic acceptance of everything in the natural world being of equal value outraged Islamic jurists who based their moral values on a strict interpretation of the Koran.

The Mevlana Tekkesi, a Sufi monastery, was founded in Konya, Turkey, in 1284 CE.

This manuscript illustration from the 11th century CE depicts a battle between Seljuk (right) and Byzantine (left) soldiers.

states in Anatolia—the sultanate of Rum (a corruption of the word *Rome*) and the Danishmend emirate—immediately threw off central authority, and the Seljuk Empire swiftly broke up. This breakup was of great advantage to the invading First Crusaders and enabled the Byzantine Empire to recover some lands in Anatolia.

The Turkic states around Palestine were in disarray until the mid-12th century CE, when, under a succession of talented leaders, they retook Jerusalem and asserted their authority over Egypt. The most notable of these leaders was Saladin, who may have been a Kurd. Saladin created his own dynasty, the Ayyubids, who were dominant in Syria

and Egypt but were unable to hold on to Persia. Here, a further Turkic state was created—the shahdom of Khoresm.

The Berber dynasties

While Turkic invaders were proving dominant within the Middle East and northern India, new non-Arab dynasties were also helping to revive Islam in northern Africa. The Berber people of northern Africa had taken some time to convert to Islam after the initial Arab conquests, but the Almoravids (a Berber dynasty) took power in Morocco in 1071 CE. The Almoravids (the name probably refers to the tightly knit groups into which the Berber warriors were organized) were fierce desert fighters. These ancestors of the modern Tuareg people of the Sahara took Islam south across the desert. The Almoravids then took over the Umayyad caliphate in Spain in 1086 CE and regained swathes of territory that Christian forces had taken after the civil war that had taken place within the Spanish caliphate early in the 11th century CE. The strength of the Almoravids lay partly in their fierce adherence to Islam, which gave them unity and a cause, but also in their military prowess. They had devised a way of fighting that their enemies had rarely encountered before. Lines of javelin throwers hurled their weapons at the foe and then pulled back to form a solid block of pikemen, who fought rather like the Macedonian phalanx or the Scottish, Flemish, and Swiss pikemen of late medieval Europe. The flanks of this block of pikemen were covered by other light troops and by cavalry mounted on camels. Horses found the camels frightening, so conventional cavalry were unable to break through on the sides of the pikemen. The camels themselves were vulnerable when they charged, but their primary purpose was defensive, and they excelled in this aspect of combat.

In the 12th century CE, the Almoravids were replaced as standard bearers of Islam in northern Africa and Spain by a second Berber dynasty, the Almohads. Originating in a call for renewal of the faith through a purer lifestyle, the Almohads extended their power from Morocco along the shores of northern Africa to as far as Tripoli in what is now Libya. They also became the leading power in Muslim Spain, supplanting the Almoravids in the 1140s CE. However, the Almohads suffered a decisive defeat by Christian armies at the battle of Las Navas de Tolosa in 1212 CE.

After that defeat, Christian forces took over large areas of southern Spain, restricting Muslim rule to the southeast, around Granada.

The coming of the Mongols

In the 13th century CE, the various states that had developed out of the ashes of the Seljuk Empire faced an enormous new threat. The Mongol forces of Genghis Khan moved out of the great plains of northeastern Asia and became the dominant political and military force over a vast area. Genghis Khan's first major campaign in the Middle East was against the Khoresm state, which he effectively destroyed by 1221 CE. The Mongols then arrived again in force in the early 1230s CE to assert their rule over Persia and Mesopotamia. Seljuk forces from Anatolia were defeated in 1243 CE at Kosedagh, and the Seljuk states there were forced to pay tribute to the Mongols. In 1256 CE, Hulagu (one of the grandsons of Genghis Khan) established the Il-Khanate, based in

This silver coin from around 1190 CE depicts the great Muslim leader Saladin.

This silver coin was issued by the Ayyubid dynasty around 1185 CE.

This practice was common within Muslim states during this period. As early as the ninth century CE, the Abbasid caliphate had recruited such children from the area between the Black and the Caspian seas.

The Mamluk children were brought up to obey a strict code called *furusiyya*, which involved obedience to their commanders, loyalty to their comrades, and generosity to women and children. They underwent constant training in the use of weapons and were expert horsemen.

The Ayyubid dynasty in Egypt, established by Saladin in the 12th century CE, became increasingly reliant on Mamluk support. During the Seventh Crusade, when Louis IX invaded Egypt, the ruling Ayyubid sultan died and a Mamluk took over. He was soon assassinated and eventually replaced by Kutuz, another Mamluk commander. Kutuz founded the Bahri dynasty, named after the Mamluk "River Island" regiment, which consisted mainly of Kipchak Turks and Circassians.

Persia, and then launched further invasions to the west. However, although Hulagu sacked Baghdad (finally extinguishing the Abbasid caliphate), the Mongols were unable to extend their rule over Egypt or much of Syria, mainly because of the resistance displayed by the rulers of Egypt, the Mamluks.

The Mamluks

The Mamluk dynasty ruled Egypt between 1250 CE and 1517 CE. More generally, however, the term *Mamluk* is used to describe a member of any number of slave armies that existed in the Islamic world in the Middle Ages. Children were received as tribute, bought as slaves, or captured, and then they were brought up as soldiers who owed complete allegiance to their ruler.

Defeat of the Mongols

In 1260 CE, the Mongol forces of Hulagu seemed invincible. They had conquered Persia, forced the Turks of Anatolia to pay them tribute, and, in 1258 CE, sacked Baghdad. However, in 1260 CE, the great khan Mangu died, and Hulagu returned to the Mongol capital of Karakorum to help elect Mangu's successor. Hulagu left a subordinate, Kitboga, in control in Syria. Kutuz attacked with a larger Egyptian force and defeated Kitboga at Ain Jalut, thanks to an ambush by Mamluks under the command of Baybars. Baybars then murdered Kutuz and took over control of Egypt. He ruled from 1260 CE to 1277 CE. Baybars was able to withstand further Mongol pressure, partly because he allied with the Mongols of the Golden Horde and through them learned about Mongol fighting methods. He undertook a successful series of campaigns against the crusader states in Palestine. After his death, the campaigns culminated in the fall of Acre in 1291 CE. The crusader states never recovered from this blow.

The Mamluk state was notoriously unstable at the top. There were 55 sultans between 1250 and 1517 CE, and fewer than 10 of these ruled for more than 12

This 13th-century-CE manuscript illustration depicts the Mongols storming Baghdad in 1288 CE.

RELIGIOUS TENSIONS

In the Middle Ages, the established Islamic world generally had a tradition of tolerance toward other religions, certainly in comparison with the Christian states of western Europe. However, outside this settled world, relationships among different religious groups were less harmonious. In Islamic Spain, for example, the Almohad dynasty, determined to impose a purer and less worldly view of Islam on the Spanish Muslims, proved intolerant of other faiths. The great flowering of Jewish culture within Islamic Spain that had begun around 1000 CE came to an abrupt end in 1148 CE, when the Almohads destroyed the Jewish communities of Andalusia. Jews were forced to flee—some to more tolerant Muslim areas such as Egypt and others to the Christian north of Spain and southern France.

years. However, the expertise of the Mamluk soldiers in mounted warfare (especially their skill with the composite bow, which the Mongols also used) made them a formidable force. They continued to resist Mongol pressure after Ain Jalut, fighting off a second Mongol invasion at the Battle of Homs in 1281 CE. The Mamluks then defeated Ghazan Khan (of the Il-Khanate) near Damascus in 1303 CE.

Almost a century later, in 1400 CE, the Mamluks were defeated by Tamerlane at the Battle of Aleppo, but fortunately for Egypt, Tamerlane moved north after this victory. Apart from extending their influence north, into Palestine, the Mamluks also attacked south. The Christian state of Maqurrah (in what is now the Sudan) was worn down by Mamluk expeditions; by 1320 CE, it had effectively become a Muslim state.

The Mongols and Islam

The spread of Islam as a religion was amply demonstrated as the 14th century CE began with the Islamization of much of the Mongol world. By 1300 CE, the rulers of the Il-Khanate in Persia had become Muslim, and the khan of the Golden Horde converted in 1313 CE. The western parts of the Jagatai Khanate of central Asia were also strongly Muslim by the time Tamerlane came to power around 1369 CE.

The conversion of the Il-Khanate was particularly important. Ghazan Khan's father had gained control of northeast Persia in 1284 CE. Brought up a Buddhist, Ghazan Khan became notable for his interest in the culture of Persia and for his knowledge of many topics that Islamic scholars had researched over the centuries, such as natural history, medicine, and astronomy. He learned various languages, including Arabic, Hindi, and Persian. His conversion to Islam came in 1295 CE, when he was campaigning against Baydu, one of his father's successors. Ghazan Khan's troops are said to have converted with him, and the fact that he now led an Islamic army is said to have contributed greatly to his success against Baydu, who was deserted by many of his Persian troops. When in power, Ghazan Khan ruled as a Persian monarch rather than as a Mongol. He specifically encouraged measures that made it more difficult for the newly arrived Mongol aristocracy to arbitrarily exact tribute from settled Persian farmers and towns. In these measures, Ghazan Khan was reflecting an important current that underlay the history of the Islamic world during this period—the conflict between the steppe nomads, who were successful militarily, and the settled agriculturalists and town dwellers, who provided the wealth that the nomads craved.

In some instances, this conflict took an obvious form: nomad armies, such as

The ancient city of Aleppo, shown here, passed through Ayyubid, Mongol, and Mamluk hands in the 13th century CE.

These glass lamps were made by Mamluk craftsmen and date to the early 14th century CE.

those of Genghis Khan, Hulagu, or Tamerlane, laid waste to entire cities. The population of Baghdad, for example was massacred twice. In 1258 CE Hulagu's troops devastated the city, and in 1401 CE, Tamerlane's forces did the same. Persia suffered greatly, and some historians claim the population dropped from more than two million to fewer than 500,000 as a result of the Mongol attacks.

However, the fate of Persia indicates how complex the relationship between the old civilizations and the violent new arrivals actually was. The Mongols and the Turkic-speaking nomads could not control the societies that they had conquered, so they became dependent upon Persian methods and individuals to rule their new empires. "The Persians ruled for a thousand years and did not need us even for a day. We have been ruling them for one or two centuries and cannot do without them for an hour," one Mongol ruler lamented. Similarly, in Egypt, the Mamluks were a nonnative military aristocracy that depended upon the agricultural riches of the Nile River and the trading expertise of Egyptian merchants for extravagant wealth and abundant military equipment.

The ghazi warriors

The conflict between, on the one hand, a sedentary culture in which peaceful relationships predominated and, on the other, a nomadic culture in which violence was accepted (and glorified) as an integral part of life was especially clear in Anatolia. After the Seljuk Turks had defeated the Byzantines at the Battle of Manzikert in 1071 CE, they had been slow to occupy the areas left defenseless. However, the Seljuk sultan was put

WHITE SHEEP AND BLACK SHEEP

Persia, which had suffered at the hands of Turkic and Mongol invaders in the 13th century CE and through the actions of Tamerlane in the 14th century CE, was invaded once again by Turkic tribes in the 15th century CE. After the death of Tamerlane in 1405 CE, various groups vied to inherit his mantle as ruler of central Asia. One was the Black Sheep Turkomans, who were initially based in what is now Azerbaijan. By the middle of the century, they had taken over much of Persia. However, they were attacked by another Turkic group, the so-called White Sheep confederacy. A three-cornered struggle followed, also involving the Safavids, another Turkic tribe based southwest of the Caspian Sea. The White Sheep Turks proved victorious, only to be brought down when they took on the rising power of the Ottoman Empire. Defeated at the Battle of Erzinjan in 1473 CE, the White Sheep Turks were eventually replaced by the Safavids. Shah Ismael I (ruled 1501–1524 CE) created a Safavid dynasty that firmly resisted any further incursions by central Asian tribes and established a secure Persian state.

under great pressure to move into Anatolia by so-called ghazi warriors—groups of Muslim Turkic fighters, often intensely religious in nature, that formed an important part of the Seljuk armies. Fierce, warlike, and brave, these men formed extremely useful irregular troops. They believed in raiding the infidel and living off the plunder they acquired. Ghazi warriors had first appeared in northern Persia, but they prospered on the borders of the Byzantine Empire during the early period of the Seljuk Empire, conducting raids on the settled farming communities of Byzantine Anatolia.

After Manzikert, the ghazis formed relatively formal brotherhoods and had their own emblem, a white cap and a club. The problem for the Seljuks was that it was impossible to control the ghazis. They were fiercely independent and resisted any form of control. Their lifestyle attracted misfits of all kinds, and because of their belief in plunder as an integral part of their livelihood, they destabilized whatever lands they lived in. If there was no frontier with the infidel for them to attack, then they tended to attack other Muslim communities. The difficulty for any authorities was that the ghazis had developed a cast-iron rationale for their activities. They represented themselves as the vanguard of the jihad (holy war), in that they were weakening the infidel by their raids, and although Islam forbade the killing of noncombatants, the ghazis believed that enslavement of captives was justified.

The coming of the Ottomans

As the Seljuk Empire broke up, the sultanate of Rum and the Danishmend emirate became dominated by ghazi brotherhoods, more so as the Mongol invasions of the 13th century CE drove ghazi fighters from Persia and central Asia to take refuge in Anatolia. By the 14th century CE, much of Muslim Anatolia was in a lawless state, with small gangs of religiously motivated fighters struggling among themselves and sometimes using the failing Byzantine Empire as an ally in these struggles. It was in this context that one particular Turkic leader, Osman, began to carve out a state for himself in western Anatolia. Osman took power in 1281 CE. From his name came the adjective *Ottoman*. Osman's small emirate would grow to become one of the greatest world empires.

See also:

The Caliphate (volume 6, page 764) • The Mongols (volume 9, page 1218) • The Rise of Islam (volume 6, page 752) • The Rise of the Ottomans (volume 9, page 1242)

The Qarawiyin Mosque in present-day Morocco was reconstructed in 1135 CE during the rule of the Almoravid dynasty.

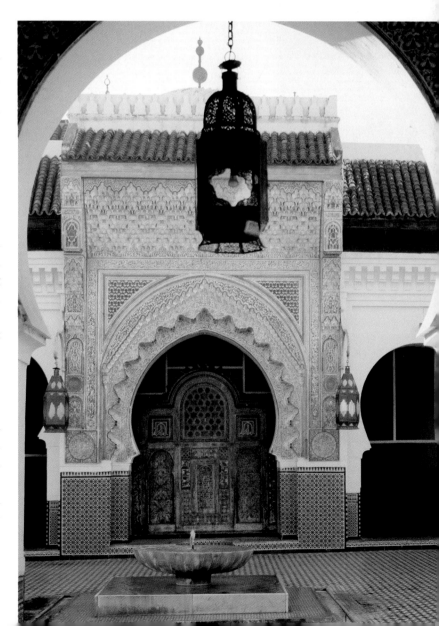

THE RISE OF THE OTTOMANS

From the 14th century CE onward, the Ottoman Turks were a huge military threat to the kingdoms of southeastern Europe. However, the Ottomans were not just fearsome soldiers; the arts and sciences flourished in the Ottoman Empire.

In the 14th and 15th centuries CE, a group of Muslim Turkic tribes from Anatolia created a great empire that endured until 1922 CE. At its height, the Ottoman Empire took in not only most of southeastern Europe but also Egypt, Israel, Syria, Iraq, the greater part of the Arabian Peninsula, and much of northern Africa. The empire took its name from Osman I (1258–1324 CE), whose Arabic name was Uthman. He laid the foundations for the empire's greatness and established the dynasty that ruled it.

The founding of an empire

Osman's father, Ertugrul (died 1280 CE), was chief of a Turkish principality based at Sogut in northwestern Anatolia. Ertugrul was descended from the Kayi, a branch of Oguz Turkmen who had fled the Turkestan region of central Asia to escape the Mongols in the early 13th century CE. According to one legend, Ertugrul dreamed that a crescent moon arose and extended from one end of the world to the other. Later, the Ottoman people, interpreting the story as a prophecy of their future greatness, adopted the crescent moon as their symbol.

Ertugrul was given control of Sogut by a Seljuk sultan. It was just one of many small states in the region to be set up by so-called ghazi warriors, who ded-icated themselves to fighting the infidel but also fought frequently among themselves. On acceding to power in Sogut, Osman captured the towns of Eskisehir, Bilecik, Yarhisar, and Yenisehir from the Byzantine Empire. He besieged the Byzantine cities of Bursa and Nicaea (modern Iznik), eventually capturing Bursa just before his death in 1324 CE. A key element in Ottoman success throughout the next 250 years was that Ottoman rulers proved very adept at taking advantage of the weaknesses of their enemies. Osman's initial expansion of his emirate took place in the context of the weakness of the Seljuks, who had been heavily defeated by the Mongols in 1243 CE and were unable to impose unified authority on Anatolia.

Osman's son Orhan (ruled 1324–1360 CE) built on his father's success. Taking advantage of the weakness of the Byzantine Empire, which had never recovered from the sacking of Constantinople by crusaders in 1204 CE, Orhan established a state in the eastern part of what had been Byzantine territory and oversaw Ottoman expansion into the Balkans. He took the city of Nicaea in 1331 CE and Nicomedia (present-day

This colored engraving from the 18th century CE depicts Osman I, the founder of the Ottoman Empire.

THE OTTOMAN EMPIRE

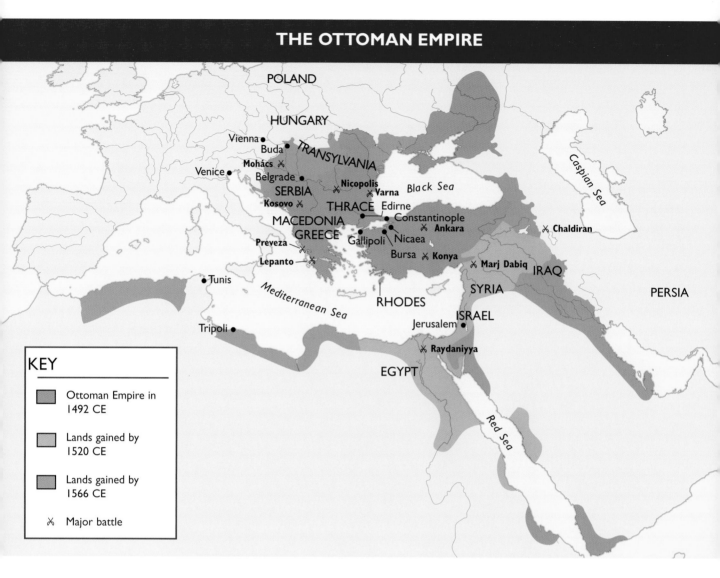

KEY

- Ottoman Empire in 1492 CE
- Lands gained by 1520 CE
- Lands gained by 1566 CE
- ⚔ Major battle

Izmit) three years later. Orhan had a strong sense of religious duty, and he developed Bursa as an Islamic center, building mosques and theological colleges. In 1345 CE, he annexed the rival Turkmen principality of Karasi in western Anatolia. In 1346 CE, Ottoman troops backed the future Byzantine emperor John VI in his struggle against a rival, John V. As a reward, Orhan received the hand in marriage of Theodora (daughter of John VI) and was given leave to conduct raids in Byzantine regions of Thrace and Macedonia. In 1354 CE, Orhan seized Gallipoli, establishing the Ottomans' first permanent holding in Europe.

Toward the end of Orhan's reign, the Ottomans acquired a navy through a daring raid carried out by Orhan's son Süleyman. One night in 1356 CE, Süleyman secretly crossed the Bosporus with an elite corps of 60 soldiers. The troops landed at Tzympe, where they sailed silently away with the Byzantine fleet. By the time the Christians had learned of their arrival, Süleyman and his men had already left. At a stroke, the Ottomans became a major naval power.

The first sultan

Although Süleyman took Tzympe and several other small territories, he never inherited the throne, because he died before his father. Instead, Orhan was succeeded in 1360 CE by another son, Murad I, the first member of the Ottoman dynasty to use the title sultan. Taking advantage of a fragile Serbian state, which had been in turmoil since the death of Stefan Dusan in 1355 CE, Murad oversaw further Ottoman expansion in the Balkans and Anatolia. In 1361 CE, he took Adrianople and Philippopolis in western Thrace and made the Byzantine emperor John V (who had regained sole power in 1354 CE) into a vassal. Murad established Adrianople as his capital and renamed it Edirne. He also established control of parts of Serbia and Bulgaria, forcing local princes to pay tribute to him. In Anatolia, he defeated a coalition of Turkmen princes at Konya in 1386 CE.

Murad developed a pragmatic method of dealing with the Christian states in the Balkans. Essentially, he left local rulers in power, provided that they paid tribute and accepted Ottoman control. Christians were not required to convert to Islam, and local customs were left alone. Murad also established a number of Ottoman institutions, such as the Janissary military corps (see box, page 1255) and the positions of grand vizier (principal minister), *beylerbeyi* (commander in chief), and *kaziasker* (military judge).

Murad died fighting Bulgarian, Serbian, and Bosnian princes at the Battle of Kosovo in 1389 CE; his son Bayezid I succeeded him as ruler.

Expanding Ottoman power

Bayezid I (ruled 1389–1402 CE) put the Ottoman Empire on a firm footing with victories in Europe and Anatolia. He was nicknamed Yildirim (Thunderbolt) for the speed of his conquests. In Europe, he occupied Tirnova (now in Bulgaria) in 1393 CE, conquered Salonika (modern Thessaloniki in Greece) in 1394 CE, and

invaded Hungary in 1395 CE—the same year that he began a siege of Constantinople. In response to the threat that the Ottomans now posed to Europe, a number of western states, including Venice and Hungary, launched a crusade. However, Bayezid defeated the alliance decisively at the Battle of Nicopolis in 1396 CE (see box, page 1248).

In Anatolia, Bayezid further expanded Ottoman territories, subduing most of the Turkmen principalities. However, this move provoked the anger of the Mongol warlord Tamerlane (also known

Murad I greatly expanded the territory under Ottoman control. He is depicted here in a 19th-century-CE watercolor.

This 16th-century-CE manuscript illustration depicts Murad I hunting for wolves.

Tamerlane did not attempt to conquer the Ottoman Empire; instead, its administration was left to Bayezid's four sons. The outcome was 10 years of civil war. The youngest son, Mehmed I (ruled 1413–1421 CE), finally brought the empire under his control by killing his brothers and fighting off both Christians and Turks in Europe and Anatolia. He died in 1421 CE and was succeeded by his 18-year-old son Murad II.

Murad II reestablished Ottoman authority in the Turkmen principalities lost to Tamerlane, and he forced the Byzantine Empire to pay tribute once again. In 1430 CE, he recaptured Salonika from the Venetians. However, he was defeated by an alliance of Hungarians, Serbians, Germans, and others at Jalowaz in 1444 CE. The defeat was only a temporary setback. Later that year, Murad inflicted a heavy defeat on an army of crusaders commanded by Wladyslaw III of Poland that had mounted a siege of the Black Sea port of Varna. This victory brought an end to western attempts to force the Ottomans out of eastern Europe and opened the way to the fall of Constantinople in 1453 CE.

In 1444 CE, before the Battle of Varna, Murad had abdicated in order to lead a life of religious devotion, and his 12-year-old son Mehmed II had temporarily taken control. Nevertheless, Murad, although no longer sultan, led the army that won this famous victory. Murad returned to the throne in 1446 CE and two years later defeated Hungarian commander János Hunyadi at the Second Battle of Kosovo. Following Murad's death in 1451 CE, Mehmed resumed his rule and set about capturing the Byzantine capital, Constantinople.

The fall of Constantinople

The city of Constantinople had long been an Ottoman target; it had been besieged five times in the previous 65

as Timur the Lame), to whom these rulers in principle owed allegiance. Tamerlane invaded Anatolia and defeated Bayezid at the Battle of Ankara in July of 1402 CE, taking the Ottoman sultan captive. Traditional accounts report that Tamerlane humiliated Bayezid by displaying him in an iron cage and by using him as a footstool. Other stories concern Bayezid's death in captivity the following year. According to some accounts, Bayezid committed suicide by beating his head against the bars of his cage. However, modern historians view these stories as inventions and believe that Bayezid was treated honorably by Tamerlane.

years. To ensure that the city finally fell into their hands, Mehmed assembled a crack army (estimated at up to 150,000 men), built a huge fleet, and ordered an enormous cannon to be cast. The siege of the city began in April of 1453 CE. At that time, the beleaguered capital of the Byzantine Empire was ruled by the young Constantine XI, whose claim to the throne was contested. Constantine also had little money and few troops. He sought help from the Christian west, but the pope was only willing to call a crusade if the Orthodox Church would merge with the Roman Church. Of all the western powers, Genoa alone responded, sending two ships to Constantine's assistance.

Although they were greatly outnumbered, the city's defenders held out valiantly for several weeks. Neither a heavy artillery bombardment nor an attempt to tunnel under the city's defenses proved successful in breaching the city's boundaries. Eventually, however, the weight of Ottoman numbers caused the Byzantine resistance to collapse.

At dawn on May 29, 1453 CE, Mehmed II, armed with an iron club, led 10,000 Janissaries in a final assault on the city. Behind them came a squad of executioners, who beheaded anyone who tried to flee. Looting began at once. Toward midday, Mehmed made a formal entry into the city, riding on horseback through the Gate of Saint Roman and symbolically proceeding into the Hagia Sophia (the Church of Holy Wisdom, built in the 6th century CE by Byzantine emperor Justinian I).

It was a momentous day. The city established as a "New Rome" and as an eastern center of the Christian faith had fallen to Muslims; henceforth, the city of Constantine would be known as Istanbul and serve as the capital of a Muslim rather than a Christian empire. Mehmed later converted the Hagia Sophia and other Christian churches into mosques.

Other triumphs

Mehmed II conquered Greece, Serbia, Bosnia, Albania, and most of the land around the Black Sea. In May of 1480 CE, he sent a fleet of 170 galleys to besiege the island of Rhodes. For once, he did not get his way; the warrior monks of the Knights Hospitallers, a brotherhood founded in Jerusalem in 1080 CE, had turned the island into an impregnable fortress. The Ottoman fleet

This 16th-century-CE Italian illustration depicts the Ottoman sultan Bayezid I.

THE BATTLE OF NICOPOLIS

In the late 14th century CE, the successes of Bayezid I and his Ottoman army in the Balkans caused considerable consternation in the west. As a result, the Byzantine emperor Manuel II and King Sigismund of Hungary persuaded the pope to call a crusade. A huge crusader army containing knights from Burgundy, England, France, Germany, and the Netherlands arrived at Buda in Hungary in July of 1396 CE. Their aim was to drive the Turks out of the Balkans and then proceed across Anatolia and Syria to Jerusalem.

The crusaders advanced across Ottoman-held Bulgaria, massacring thousands of locals—Muslims and Christians—along the way. The crusaders then besieged Nicopolis, the principal Ottoman garrison on the Danube River. Bayezid abandoned his own siege of Constantinople and marched to drive the Christian force from Nicopolis. The speed of Bayezid's response took the crusaders by surprise.

On September 25, the crusaders attacked Bayezid's men. The main section of the Ottoman army was based largely on the top of a hill. Ignoring the advice of their ally Mircea the Elder (the ruler of Wallachia), the heavily armored French and English knights charged up the hill but were forced to dismount by a line of defensive stakes. Upon reaching the top, the exhausted crusaders were slaughtered by the Ottomans, who went on to win the battle.

A small contingent under Sigismund escaped, but the great majority of the surviving crusaders were captured and put to death by Bayezid. The sultan's victory consolidated the Ottomans' already strong position in the Balkans, while keeping up pressure on the beleaguered Byzantine Empire.

In this 19th-century-CE illustration, Sigismund is being rescued after the Battle of Nicopolis.

besieged the island for more than three months and made three unsuccessful attempts to take it. The Ottomans abandoned the siege in August, having lost 9,000 men in the engagement.

Mehmed's military successes won him the nickname Conqueror, but he was also a well-educated man and an able administrator who rebuilt Constantinople and promulgated the Kanun Nameh, a codification of Ottoman law. He oversaw the compilation of a tax register, in which *beys* (district administrators) recorded the values and sources of their income, tax rates, and penalties. He also established a group of advisers called the *ulama* (Arabic for "wise"). These men had all mastered three languages: Turkish, Arabic, and Persian. They were also expert interpreters of the Islamic holy book—the Koran, from which all matters of law and science were derived in the Ottoman Empire.

The empire that Mehmed created was notable for its religious tolerance, and the major religious groups in the empire had their own form of self-government. This policy paid great dividends. For example, when Mehmed invaded Bosnia, the local Bogomil Christians helped the Ottoman forces against the Catholic army of Hungary.

Bayezid II

Mehmed was succeeded by his son Bayezid II in 1481 CE. Bayezid had outmaneuvered his brother Cem to gain the throne, and Cem had fled. Cem fell into the hands of the Knights Hospitallers and remained in captivity for the rest of his life. Over the course of the next three decades, Bayezid further consolidated the empire, winning great successes against Hungary, Poland, Venice, and the Safavid rulers of Persia.

Bayezid was a learned and pious Muslim, and he poured funds into the building of bridges, hospitals, mosques, and theological colleges within the empire. He promoted law, learning, and poetry, and he took a deep interest in cosmology and philosophy.

In 1511 CE, Bayezid faced a revolt by his sons, Selim and Ahmed, who were also fierce rivals of one other. In April of 1512 CE, having lost the support of the Janissaries, Bayezid was forced to abdicate. He was succeeded by Selim.

Selim I

Selim I (ruled 1512–1520 CE), who was also known as Yavuz (the Grim), established the Ottomans as the leading power

This 19th-century-CE watercolor depicts the Ottoman sultan Murad II, who helped reestablish Ottoman authority in Anatolia.

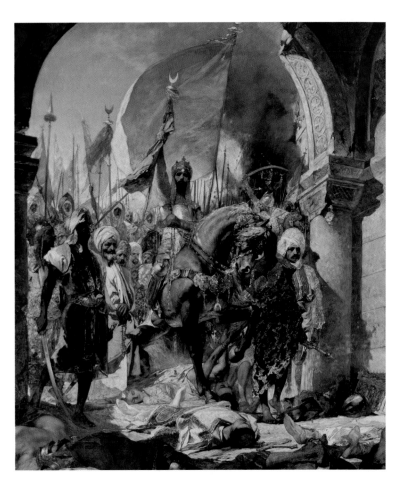

This 19th-century-CE painting depicts the Ottoman sultan Mehmed II entering Constantinople after its fall in 1453 CE.

in the Muslim world. He first secured the succession, doing away with all possible claimants to the throne, save his son Süleyman. He then attacked Ismael I, the founder of the Safavid dynasty in Persia (modern Iran), which posed a threat to Ottoman stability. Selim saw the Safavid regime as heretical; the Ottomans were followers of mainstream Sunni Islam, while Ismael espoused the Shi'ite form of the religion. At the same time, the Turkmen Kizilbash people, who proclaimed loyalty to Ismael, rose in revolt in Anatolia. Selim crushed the Kizilbash rebellion and then unleashed his cannons to annihilate Ismael at the Battle of Chaldiran, which took place by the Euphrates River on August 23, 1514 CE. Selim then brought the Kurdish and Turkmen principalities in Anatolia into the Ottoman Empire.

GOVERNING THE EMPIRE

By the time of Süleyman I's reign (1520–1566 CE), Ottoman government was organized into four branches or institutions: imperial, military, scribal, and religious. The imperial institution had two sub-branches: an inner service to deal with palace matters and an outer service that had a regulatory function. The military institution, led by the Janissaries and the cavalry, was responsible for defense of the empire and conquest of new territories.

Administration of the empire was the province of the scribal institution. Süleyman established 21 virtually independent provinces, which were in turn divided into 250 *sanchaks* (financial administrative districts). The *sanchaks* were run by an administrative civil service with the authority to collect taxes.

The payment of tax was required of all Muslims. Intended to help the poor, especially with health care and education, tax revenues also paid the ransoms of Ottomans taken prisoner in war, the costs of waging war, and inducements to encourage people of other faiths to convert to Islam.

The religious institution was responsible for Islamic guidance, education, and the administration of justice. *Islam* is the Arabic word for "surrender," and Islamic religious law and ethics (*sharia*) assume a willingness to surrender to the will of Allah and to meet social obligations. However, Süleyman did not insist that his subjects convert to Islam; Christians and Jews were free to practice their own religions as long as they paid a special tax (*jizyah*).

In 1516 CE, Selim launched an attack on the Mamluk Empire of Syria, Palestine, Egypt, and Arabia. The word *Mamluk* means "slave" in Arabic, and the Mamluks were originally enslaved Kipchak Turks (and others) from the area of the Black and Caspian seas. Those slaves were in the service of the Egyptian ruler, but in 1250 CE, they had rebelled and created their own government and empire. Although individually the Mamluks were fearsome warriors, the Ottoman armies were well organized tactically and their use of cannons was

This medieval manuscript illustration depicts the Ottoman naval assault on Rhodes in 1480 CE.

The reign of Süleyman I proved to be a golden age for Ottoman culture. He is depicted here in a 16th-century-CE illustration.

extremely effective. Selim defeated the Mamluks in two great battles—at Marj Dabiq (near Aleppo in Syria) on August 24, 1516 CE, and at Raydaniyya (near Cairo) on January 22, 1517 CE. Syria, Egypt, and Palestine were then subject to Ottoman rule.

Süleyman I

Süleyman I succeeded his father, Selim, in 1520 CE and reigned until 1566 CE.

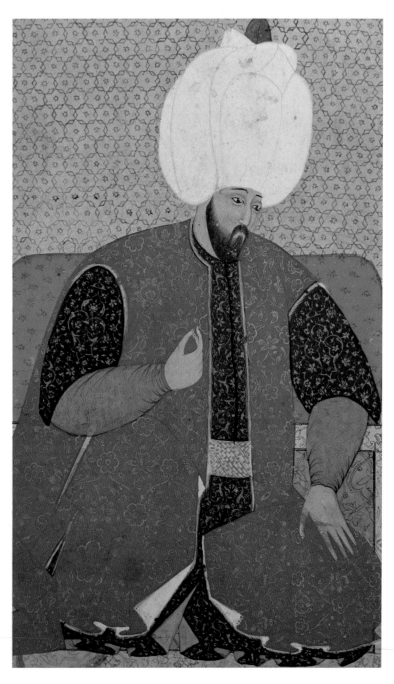

In the course of his 46-year rule, he brought the Ottoman Empire to its peak, crossing the Danube River to take Hungary, seizing the area of Anatolia that remained outside Ottoman influence, and capturing parts of Iraq. His realm ran from the Balkans to the Middle East and Persia; in Arabia, it included the coasts of the Red Sea and the Persian Gulf.

On land, Süleyman fought repeatedly in Hungary. He first invaded in 1521 CE, seizing the city of Belgrade (then a possession of the Hungarians). When Süleyman returned in 1526 CE, he killed the Hungarian king, Louis II, and defeated the Hungarian army at the Battle of Mohács. In 1529 CE, he supported John Zápolya, the lord of Transylvania who had been elected king by Hungarian nobles, against a challenger, Austria's Hapsburg archduke Ferdinand I. Süleyman drove Ferdinand back into Vienna and then unsuccessfully besieged the city. Following John Zápolya's death in 1540 CE, the Austrians invaded Hungary again, provoking Süleyman to take action once more. He captured Buda (across the Danube from the city of Pest, and now part of the Hungarian capital Budapest) and incorporated the middle Danube region into the Ottoman Empire, leaving the Hapsburgs in control in northern Hungary and allowing Transylvania limited freedom as a vassal state under the rule of John Zápolya's son John Sigismund.

Süleyman also fought three campaigns against the Safavid dynasty of Persia between 1534 CE and 1555 CE, during the course of which he captured Iraq. He signed a peace treaty with the Safavids in 1555 CE.

Mediterranean campaigns

At sea, Süleyman's fleet came to dominate the Mediterranean region. In 1522 CE, he drove the Knights Hospitallers from the island of Rhodes, 42 years after

ADMIRAL BARBAROSSA

Under the leadership of the great admiral Khayr ad-Din (c. 1478–1546 CE), the Ottoman navy achieved a position of dominance in the Mediterranean Sea. That position lasted from the 1530s CE until the navy's defeat at the Battle of Lepanto in 1571 CE, a quarter of a century after the death of Khayr ad-Din. The admiral, originally called Khidr, was given the name Khayr ad-Din (Greatness of the Faith) by Süleyman I. In the west, Khayr ad-Din was known as Barbarossa (Red Beard). This nickname derived from the name Baba Oruç, which he had taken on when his elder brother died; to Europeans, the name sounded like Barbarossa. In any case, it was an apt nickname, because Khayr ad-Din did indeed have a red beard.

Khayr ad-Din was born on the Aegean island of Midilli (present-day Lesbos). He was the son of a knight who had fought for Mehmed II in the capture of the island from the Genoese in 1462 CE and then stayed there. Khayr ad-Din began life sailing as a privateer, capturing Algiers in 1516 CE. The island became part of the Ottoman Empire. In 1529 CE, Süleyman made Khayr ad-Din the Ottomans' admiral-in-chief, and in 1534 CE, he captured Tunis for the empire. In 1535 CE, Holy Roman Emperor Charles V recaptured Tunis. However, in 1538 CE, Khayr ad-Din won a major victory over Charles's fleet at the Battle of Preveza. The victory assured Ottoman dominance in the Mediterranean. In 1540 CE, Charles tried to persuade Khayr ad-Din to abandon the Ottomans and serve the Holy Roman Empire instead, offering him the position

This 19th-century-CE French portrait of Khayr ad-Din is a lithograph based on an earlier original.

of admiral-in-chief and possession of all Spain's territories in northern Africa. Barbarossa refused.

Khayr ad-Din continued to terrorize western-held islands and coastal possessions on the Mediterranean until he retired to Istanbul in 1545 CE. He built a palace on the Bosporus shore but died the following year.

This 16th-century-CE manuscript illustration depicts the siege of Belgrade by Ottoman forces. Belgrade fell to the Ottomans in 1521 CE.

they had defied the invasion attempt of Mehmed II. Süleyman unleashed 400 ships carrying an army of 200,000 men against a defending force of 7,000. Despite this inequality of numbers, the siege lasted six months. The Ottomans finally prevailed, however. Süleyman was generous in victory, allowing the survivors among the defenders to leave Rhodes for Malta, which was part of the kingdom of Sicily at that point.

A series of strategically important naval victories followed. At the Battle of Preveza, fought off the Greek coast in 1538 CE, an Ottoman fleet defeated a combined force from Spain, Genoa, Venice, the Papal States, and Malta. The victory gave the Ottomans control of the eastern Mediterranean region. Süleyman's domain eventually reached to northern Africa, where he captured Tripoli in 1551 CE and defeated a Spanish campaign in 1560 CE.

JANISSARIES

The elite Ottoman military unit of the Janissaries was established by Murad I in the 14th century CE. The unit's name is a Latin corruption of the Turkish *yeni cheri*, meaning "new army." Murad used unconventional methods of recruitment for his army; he demanded Christian children from Balkan provinces as tribute, put them in training camps, and indoctrinated them in Islam. This method of recruitment, called *devshirme* (from the Turkish for "gathering"), was common throughout the 15th and 16th centuries CE. The Janissaries, eventually numbering 40,000, played a large part in the success of the Ottoman Empire. They did, however, represent a risk; in the 17th and 18th centuries CE, a Janissary revolt was always enough to bring down a sultan.

The Janissary corps was abolished in 1826 CE. Janissaries attempted to revolt in that year, and the sultan, Mahmud II, unleashed a cannonade on their barracks. Most members of the elite corps were killed, and the remainder were disbanded.

Government and culture

Süleyman was called "the Magnificent" abroad, but at home, he was known as "the Just" or "the Lawgiver" because of his development of the legal system of Mehmed II. He appointed very able statesmen and religious advisers—grand viziers (ministers) such as Rustem and *ulama* such as Kemalpasazade. Another trusted advisor was Roxelana, one of Süleyman's wives.

Süleyman had total authority over imperial resources. He acquired huge estates from the rulers he vanquished in the course of his conquests, and then he leased them to his followers—vassals with essentially no independent political power. Under the Islamic laws of inheritance, women were not permitted to come into possession of land, so when a family of vassals died out, the estates reverted to the sultan.

Süleyman was a great patron of architecture, and he was given the epithet "the Magnificent" because of the sacred and secular buildings he had built in Istanbul and in other cities of the empire. In particular, he oversaw the design and construction of several of the superb creations by the architect Mimar Sinan. They included the Sehzade Mosque and the Mosque of Süleyman in Istanbul and the Selim Mosque in Edirne—all of which are considered to be masterpieces. Süleyman was also a great patron of other arts, including poetry. The sultan financially supported a large number of artistic societies; records reveal that at any one time up to 600 artists and craftsmen could be employed by the palace.

Süleyman the Magnificent died on September 5, 1566 CE, while on campaign in Hungary. He was succeeded by his son Selim II.

See also:

Turkish Empires and the Islamic World (volume 9, page 1230)

AFRICA'S EARLY CULTURES

TIME LINE

c. 4 million BCE
Early hominids emerge in eastern and southern Africa.

c. 2 million BCE
Homo habilis and *Homo erectus* evolve.

c. 100,000 BCE
First modern humans develop in Africa.

c. 15,000 BCE
Bows and arrows first used in Africa.

c. 2000 BCE
Bronze Age begins in northern Africa.

c. 1800 BCE
Previously fertile Sahara becomes desert.

c. 1000 BCE
Copper industry flourishes in southern Congo.

c. 700 BCE
Iron Age begins in Egypt.

c. 200 CE
Iron Age methods spread to eastern and central Africa.

Africa was the cradle of civilization. The earliest humans emerged on the continent in prehistory and gradually populated all habitable parts of the landmass. They also developed a wide range of languages and traditions.

The earliest humans in Africa evolved primarily in the eastern central and southern parts of the continent. Around four million years ago, a hominid (forerunner of humans) known as *Australopithecus* (southern ape) lived in those regions and perhaps elsewhere. Archaeologists have found australopithecine skeletons in Ethiopia and South Africa. Unlike their apelike ancestors, who moved on all fours, australopithecine beings walked on two legs. They were up to 4.5 feet (1.4 m) tall and had brains that were 35 percent the size of modern human brains.

Around two million years ago, *Homo habilis* (skilled man) and *Homo erectus* (upright man) evolved. Skeletal remains of the two groups dating from 1.7–1.8 million years ago have been found in Tanzania and Kenya. *Homo erectus* was around 5 feet 10 inches (1.79 m) tall and had brains that were 75 percent the size of modern human brains. *Homo sapiens* (thinking man) emerged around one million years ago and gradually evolved into *Homo sapiens sapiens*, the earliest modern human, who appeared around 100,000 BCE. The oldest identifiably human remains, dating from around 120,000–90,000 BCE, have been unearthed in Ethiopia and Tanzania and on the border between Swaziland and South Africa.

Hunter-gatherers

The earliest *Homo sapiens sapiens* lived by hunting and gathering. They hunted gazelle, eland, and quagga (a species of zebra, now extinct) and foraged for grubs and plants. They traveled great distances in small family groups, camping in caves or beneath small clumps of trees. They used stone tools, and they were making bows and arrows by around 15,000 BCE. (Some inhabitants of the region—notably the Khoikhoi and the San in the Kalahari Desert—have maintained this lifestyle into the 21st century CE.)

In the equatorial rain forests of the Congo River Basin, other groups of hunter-gatherers emerged. Among them were the Twa and the Mbuti, diminutive humans with an average height of 5 feet (1.5 m). Their descendants remain there in the modern era. (Genetically distinct non-African pygmies, probably also of archaic origin, live in Asia and Oceania.)

Growth of agriculture

Around 13,000 BCE, climate changes in northern Africa caused desertification and led to a sharp decline in the number and variety of wild animals. The human population of the region responded by developing a new culture based on the gathering of wild grains, which they threshed with stone sickles and crushed with grinding stones. The culture spread

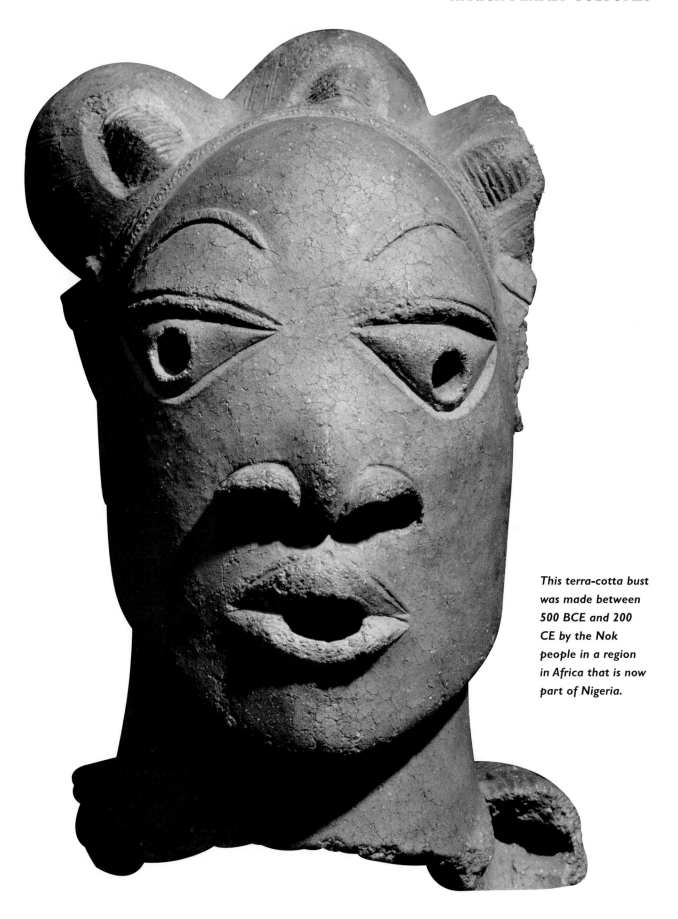

This terra-cotta bust was made between 500 BCE and 200 CE by the Nok people in a region in Africa that is now part of Nigeria.

PEOPLES OF AFRICA

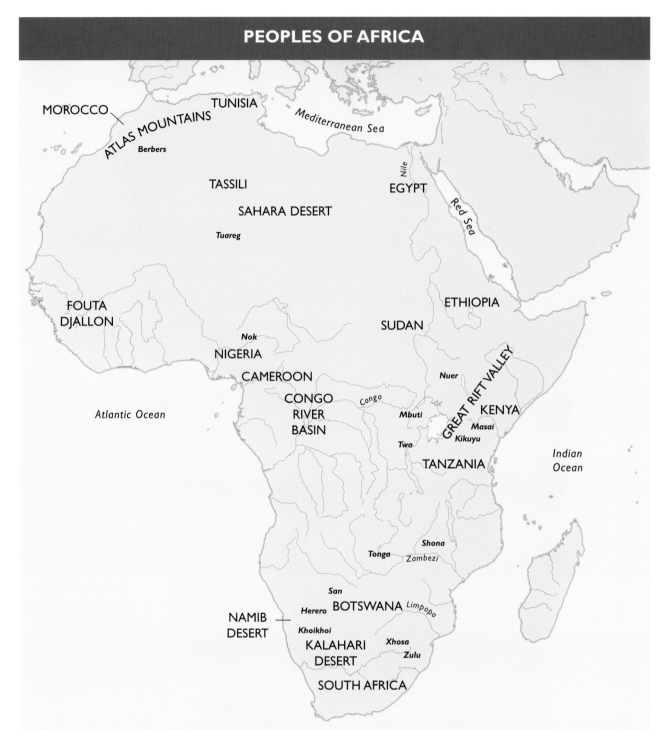

through northern Africa and along the eastern coast of the Mediterranean Sea into Palestine, Syria, Mesopotamia, and Persia. In an effort to regularize their supply of food, the indigenous peoples began to raise plants and domesticate goats, sheep, cattle, and donkeys. The same period saw the emergence of the Afro-Asiatic family of languages, a group that includes the Coptic (ancient Egyptian) and Semitic tongues.

Later, from around 9000 to 2000 BCE, there was a prolonged period of abundant rainfall in eastern Africa. As a result, the region was distinctly different from the desert that covers much of it today; the landscape was characterized by wooded hills, green valleys, and wide rolling plains. The topography engendered a water-based culture that spread across northern Africa from the Atlantic Ocean to the Nile River and south to the lake country in eastern Africa. Around 8000 BCE, hunters and gatherers yielded the most fertile areas of Africa to peoples who had developed new techniques of agriculture and animal husbandry. Those peoples, who spoke languages of the Nile-Saharan group, also manufactured pottery. They lived mainly in encampments, which they used for gathering seasonal crops or hunting, but they also had some permanent settlements. In the Tassili region of the central Sahara, these peoples left thousands of wall paintings that depicted their lifestyle. The primitive art provides much valuable information about the people's methods of herding and hunting (particularly gazelles, giraffes, and elephants) and their rituals, which featured music and dancing.

The period of abundant rainfall ended around 2000 BCE, and within 200 years, the greater part of northern Africa had been transformed into a vast desert. As the region's inhabitants adapted to the hotter and drier environment, they concentrated on the crops that produced the greatest food yield for the least physical work. The particular crops varied by region.

Social organization

Studies of present-day hunter-gatherer groups by anthropologists have yielded valuable clues to the social organization of their prehistoric African forebearers.

*This **Homo erectus** skull, dating from between 2.1 and 1.3 million years ago, was discovered in 1959 CE in the region around Lake Turkana, Kenya.*

In light of the research, it is likely that the early hunter-gatherers had strong social bonds designed to maintain group identity. Their core values were equality and communal sharing. Decisions were reached by negotiation rather than imposed from above by leaders. The hunting was probably carried out by the men, and the foraging was performed by the women. Because hunting was considered more important than gathering, the men were accorded higher social status.

With the transition to an agrarian lifestyle, new social structures probably evolved in order to manage the larger groups living in permanent or semipermanent settlements. Groups of people were probably identified on the basis of collective identity as descendants of a common ancestor. Genealogy was traced either from a male ancestor (patrilineal

AFRICA'S GEOGRAPHY AND TOPOGRAPHY

The continent of Africa occupies 11.7 million square miles (30 million km²), one-fifth of Earth's total land area. To the west, it is bounded by the Atlantic Ocean, to the east by the Red Sea and the Indian Ocean, to the north by the Mediterranean Sea, and to the south by the confluence of the Atlantic and the Indian oceans off the Cape of Good Hope. Africa contains a wide variety of terrains, ranging from tropical forest to desert, from snowcapped mountain ranges to vast, flat savannahs.

Africa is divided into three main regions: the Northern Plateau, the Eastern Highlands, and the Central and Southern Plateau. The bulk of the Northern Plateau is occupied by the Sahara, a desert that covers 3.5 million square miles (9 million km²), more than one-quarter of the continent. To the northwest, the desert gives way to semiarid steppes and the rugged peaks of the Atlas Mountains in Morocco and Tunisia. To the southwest lie the Fouta Djallon highlands, and to the south lie the mountains of Cameroon.

The fertile plateau of the Eastern Highlands runs down the eastern coast of Africa, from the Red Sea to the Zambezi River. The plateau is the highest part of the continent, with an average elevation of more than 5,000 feet (1,500 m). The Great Rift Valley, running 3,000 miles (4,830 km) from Syria to southeastern Africa, cuts through the Eastern Highlands. The Nile River—which, at 4,132 miles (6,650 km), is the longest river in the world—rises in the Eastern Highlands and flows northward to the Mediterranean through a chain of lakes in the Great Rift Valley.

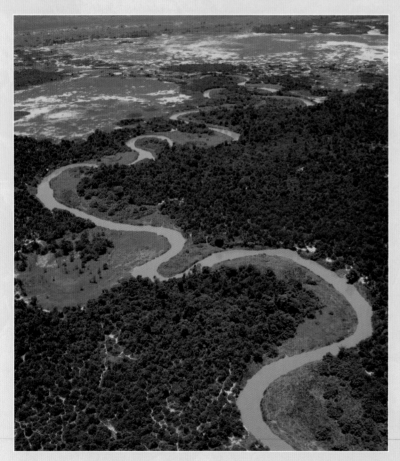

The Central and Southern Plateau, which covers most of western central and southern Africa, contains the Congo River and the Kalahari Desert. The Congo River Basin consists of more than 1.6 million square miles (4.1 million km²) of dense equatorial rain forest. The Kalahari Desert covers 275,000 square miles (712,250 km²). It is mostly arid red soil, although there are expanses of sand in the east. West of the Kalahari, the temperate Namib Desert extends 1,200 miles (1,930 km) along the southwestern coast of Africa. The Namib is cooled by the offshore Benguela Current. In the extreme south, the High Veld is an arid area that covers much of South Africa.

The Rwindi River is part of the massive drainage system of the Congo River Basin.

descent) or from a female ancestor (matrilineal descent). As lineage began to play a more important role in the organization of food production and society, leaders—and especially the elderly—were accorded higher status than other members of the group. Marriage arrangements became important economic and political factors.

The spread of metalworking

In many parts of the world, human evolution progressed from the Stone Age (during which people made tools from stone), through the Bronze Age (when tools and weapons were made of bronze, an alloy of copper and tin), to the Iron Age (when iron was used). In Africa, however, development did not always conform to the same pattern. Although bronze was made and used to a limited degree in northern Africa around 2000 BCE and there was a flourishing copper industry in southern Congo at the start of the first millennium BCE, the continent as a whole did not pass through a Bronze Age; it generally moved straight from stone to iron.

By around 700 BCE, iron was already in use in the lower reaches of the Nile River (the northern part of modern Egypt), to which it had been brought by the Assyrians, and in Carthage (a city in modern Tunisia), to which it had been brought by the Phoenicians. Africa's earliest indigenous ironmaking culture was that of the Nok in central Nigeria (c. 500 BCE–200 CE). Nok artisans were renowned for their life-size terra-cotta sculptures in addition to their iron artifacts (see box, page 1263). Subsequently, from around 200 CE, the use of iron became widespread among other cultures in eastern and central Africa.

This painting of dancers dates from around 5000 BCE. It was found on the wall of a cave in the Tassili region of the Sahara Desert.

SAN ROCK PAINTINGS

The San bushmen, who now live in the Kalahari Desert, created a major legacy in painted and carved rock art at around 50,000 sites across most of the southern half of Africa. The San roamed freely over a vast region for thousands of years before they were largely confined to the Kalahari Desert by Bantu settlers around 400 CE. There are major concentrations of San art in the Drakensberg Mountains in South Africa, in the Matobo Hills in Zimbabwe, in the Tsodilo Hills in Botswana, and at Twyfelfontein in Namibia.

Some examples of San art are extremely old. One rock in the shape of a snake and cut with marks that look like scales may date from 75,000 BCE. Slabs of rock painted in charcoal, white, and ocher were found in a cave in the Hun Mountains of southwestern Namibia and were dated to 25,000 BCE. At one time, these paintings, which show both animals and humans, were believed to be scenes of everyday life, but they are now thought to be religious paintings made by shamans (tribal spirit guides or religious leaders). The shamans would have used the images to record visions they had in the spirit world and to bring their people into contact with supernatural forces. The shamans and their followers believed that the images had the power to promote rainfall, bring healing to the sick, or deliver prey to the hunters. Depicted animals include the eland, the hippopotamus, the elephant, and the giraffe. The pictures rarely represented the kinds of animals that the San bushmen habitually ate, such as tortoises and small antelopes.

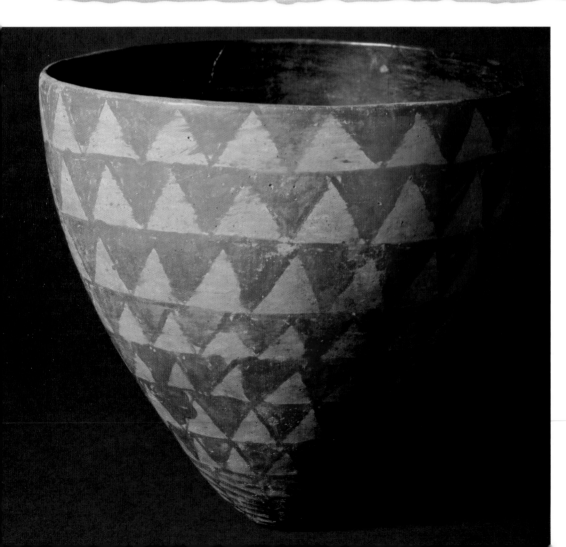

Measuring 8 inches (20 cm) in height, this clay bowl was made by Nubian peoples of the Nile River around 3000 BCE.

Made around 40,000 years ago, these hand axes were unearthed on the banks of a lake in Botswana.

During the first four centuries of the Common Era, the practices developed by the early agrarian and Iron Age societies spread, through human migration, to other parts of Africa. The migrants organized themselves into units of increasing size, and political leaders became more and more important as early African kingdoms developed.

Bantu migrations

Through the study of African languages (see box, page 1264), historians have hypothesized that a vast migration of speakers of Bantu languages took place over the course of hundreds of years, beginning in the first millennium BCE and continuing until around 400 CE. The evidence suggests that the Bantu moved south from their original home-land in the lower Niger region and di-vided into eastern and western branches. The eastern Bantu migrated through what is now Zimbabwe, crossing the

THE NOK CULTURE

The Nok culture existed on Nigeria's Benue Plateau from around 500 BCE to around 200 CE. The culture was characterized by superb life-size terra-cotta statues of people and animals. Unfortunately, most of the statues survive only in fragments. The culture takes its name from the village of Nok, where the first terra-cotta pieces were unearthed during tin-mining operations in 1928 CE. Four years later, 11 statues in immaculate condition were discovered near Sokoto in northwestern Nigeria. Other remains were subsequently found over a wide area, and the culture is believed to have extended over a region measuring 200 miles (320 km) north to south and 300 miles (480 km) east to west. The Nok artisans exhibited extraordinary skill in their modeling. Some of their statues were more than 4 feet (1.2 m) tall. The statues have well-defined characteristics and few stylistic differences. These facts suggest that the modelers may have been working in a well-established artistic tradition whose earlier manifestations are lost. The artisans also made iron tools (among the first in Africa), as well as stone ornaments and stone tools (including axes).

THE SPREAD OF AFRICAN LANGUAGES AND CULTURE

Today, there are more than 1,000 languages in Africa. Most of them are spoken by no more than 200,000 people, although 50 languages are used by more than 500,000 people. Writing systems exist for only around one-half of these languages, which have no early literature but are noted for their ancient oral traditions. Their alphabets were created in the 19th century CE by Christian missionaries, who adapted the Roman alphabet to the sounds they encountered. On the basis of the spread and development of languages, historians have traced the development of African cultures and the movement of peoples. The four principal groups of African languages are Afro-Asiatic (Hamito-Semitic), Nilo-Saharan, Niger-Kordofanian, and Khoisan.

The Afro-Asiatic (Hamito-Semitic) family includes the ancient Egyptian language, written in hieroglyphics, and Tamarshak, spoken by the Berbers of the Atlas Mountains and the Tuareg of the Sahara. As the name suggests, Nilo-Saharan languages developed in the upper valley of the Nile River, the Sudan, the Sahara, and eastern Africa. A key subgroup is the Nilotic languages, which are spoken by two large cattle-based cultures—the Nuer and the Masai.

The Niger-Kordofanian group is the largest of the four language families of Africa. The group includes the languages of the Bantu peoples. Niger-Kordofanian languages are divided into two subgroups: the Niger-Congo family and the Kordofanian family. The Niger-Congo languages spread across virtually all of Africa south of the Sahara; the Kordofanian languages, which include Swahili, are used only in southern Sudan.

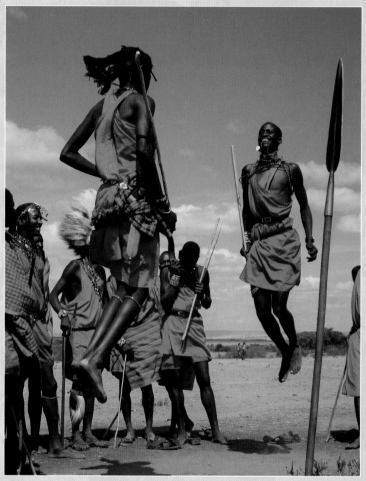

The Masai are a mainly pastoralist people who live along the Great Rift Valley of Kenya and Tanzania and speak a Nilotic language.

Khoisan, the language of the Khoikhoi and San hunter-gatherer peoples, is the smallest of the African language families. It is sometimes called the click language, because it is characterized by distinctive clicking sounds made with the tongue. Khoisan is spoken today by around 100,000 people, primarily the Khoikhoi and San of southern Africa. The click has spread through cultural and linguistic contact into a number of Bantu languages, including Xhosa, Zulu, and Sotho in South Africa and Dahalo in Kenya.

Limpopo River into South Africa. Their descendants include the Kikuyu, Shona, Xhosa, and Zulu peoples. The western Bantu moved down the Atlantic coast and then inland to become the ancestors of the Herero and Tonga peoples.

The Bantu were pastoralists, herders, and cattle breeders. Their advanced techniques of farming and ironmaking enabled them to dominate the cultures they encountered. They probably learned their ironmaking techniques from the people of the Nok culture. It is possible that the spread of Bantu languages was caused not by a vast human migration but rather by a cross-fertilization of culture through a small number of travelers or by intermarriage.

As they or their culture spread, the Bantu displaced the indigenous hunter-gatherer peoples of the Khoikhoi and the San. Both peoples adopted aspects of the Bantu culture but retained their own language, Khoisan.

These Bantu warriors were photographed in Congo in 1894 CE.

See also:

The Rise and Fall of African Empires
(volume 9, page 1266)

THE RISE AND FALL OF AFRICAN EMPIRES

During a period that lasted for almost 900 years, Africa saw a succession of kingdoms and empires that were almost invariably self-governed by the native populations. That period was ended by the start of European colonialism in the 19th century CE.

After 1000 CE, a series of regional kingdoms and empires rose and fell in Africa. Most of them were founded on the wealth generated by long-distance trade. Many grew into great civilizations, whose craftspeople developed sophisticated skills in working clay, stone, and metal.

Nubia

The first great civilization of tropical Africa was the kingdom of Nubia, which was created around 1000 BCE by the peoples of the middle part of the Nile River Valley (now part of Sudan). The area, a major source of gold, had previously been dominated for 1,800 years by the Egyptians, who called it the Land of Kush. In the eighth century BCE, the Nubian king Shabaka conquered Egypt and established the 25th dynasty of pharaohs, who held power for around 50 years. However, in 671 BCE, the Assyrians attacked Egypt, seizing control of the empire and driving the Nubians back to the Land of Kush.

From the Assyrians, the Nubians learned how to make iron. The first capital of the Nubian kingdom had been established on a bend of the Nile River at Napata, around 250 miles (400 km) north of Khartoum, an area rich in iron ore. By the sixth century BCE, however, the region was becoming overexploited; there was little wood left for burning to smelt iron ore. Consequently, Napata was replaced as the capital by Meroë, a site farther up river, only around 125 miles (200 km) north of Khartoum.

The Nubians controlled major trade routes along which they sold iron, gold, ivory, and elephants—not only in Africa but also to Greece and Rome. The kingdom's power increased in direct proportion to its wealth. In 24 BCE, the Nubians destroyed two Egyptian outposts of the Roman Empire, at Philae and Aswan, thereby forcing a border agreement between Nubia and Roman Egypt. (The Greek historian Strabo later wrote that the assault on Philae had been made by a "Queen Candace," but he had mistranslated Candace, a Nubian word for queen rather than a personal name; the word merely indicated that a female ruler had led the attack.)

The power and influence of Nubia in the first century CE is evidenced by its exchange of ambassadors with the Roman emperor Nero (ruled 54–68 CE). Its heyday was brief, however. The Nubian Empire soon crumbled, losing much of its territory to desert nomads, notably the Blemmyes of the Arabian Desert. Around 350 CE, Meroë was overrun by Ezana, king of Aksum, a realm on the Ethiopian Plateau.

The people of Nubia were converted to Christianity in the sixth century CE

This 18th-century-CE bust, made of gold, is an outstanding example of Ashanti metalwork.

This scene, painted on the side of a wooden casket in the tomb of the pharaoh Tutankhamen (ruled 1332–1323 BCE), depicts an Egyptian battle against the Nubians.

and proceeded to establish the kingdoms of Nobatia, Mukurra, and Alodia. All three realms were conquered by Arabs in the 14th century CE, although Alodia resisted until the 16th century CE. Egypt regained control of the former Nubian region in 1820 CE.

Aksum

The ancient kingdom of Aksum, in the northern Ethiopian highlands, was founded around 50 CE by the Amhara, a people of partly Semitic origin. The rulers of Aksum established the Solomonid dynasty, which claimed descent from the biblical king Solomon.

According to legend, the people of Sabaea, a Semitic kingdom of southern Arabia, had migrated across the Red Sea to Ethiopia at the start of the first millennium BCE. Their ruler, Makeda (the biblical queen of Sheba), was said to have known Solomon (a 10th-century-BCE king of Israel) and borne him a son, who became Menelik I ("Emperor and King of Kings of Ethiopia" and the ancestor of the Solomonid rulers). All Ethiopian emperors claim descent from Menelik in the royal line of the Lion of Judah.

The Aksumite Empire was established by 100 CE. The foundation of its commercial success was ivory, of which it had an abundant supply. From its main port, Adulis (modern Massawa) on the Red Sea, Aksum forged strong trading links with Greece, Rome, and India. Many of the proceeds were spent on the construction of great palaces and temples. From the third century CE to the sixth century CE, Aksum also dominated Yemen on the Arabian Peninsula.

In the fourth century CE, Ezana of Aksum (the king who overran Meroë in Nubia) made Christianity one of the state religions—after he himself had been converted by two Syrian Christians, Frumentius and Aedesius. Surrounded at first by pagans and then by Muslims, the Aksumite Empire fought wars for religious as well as economic reasons. In the seventh century CE, Aksum declined, but its kings retained power through alliances with the Byzantine Empire. In the 10th century CE, the Solomonid dynasty was toppled by the Zagwe, the ruling family of Lasta, a kingdom of the Central Plateau region.

Ghana

In western Africa, a succession of states became rich and powerful through their control of trade routes across the Sahara. Ghana, the region's first great empire, grew up around 400 CE out of the Iron Age culture of the Nok people. The empire lay between the upper Senegal River and the Niger River, northwest of the modern country of Ghana. Extending from Timbuktu on the Niger to the Atlantic Ocean, ancient Ghana was well positioned for trade. Its lands roughly covered what is now eastern Senegal, western Mali, and southeastern Mauritania.

The empire—known locally at the time as Wagadou (Land of Herds)—later became known as Ghana because that was the word for "king" in the Wagadou language. Ghana prospered most between the 8th and 11th centuries CE. Its gold, mined in the Wangara region in

This photograph shows the pyramids at Meroë, Sudan, the ancient capital of the Nubian Empire.

THE CAPITAL OF THE GHANA EMPIRE

The capital of the Ghana Empire was described in *The Book of Roads and Kingdoms*, written around 1068 CE by El Bekri, a geographer from Córdoba, Spain. He wrote: "Ghana consists of two cities situated on a plain. One, inhabited by Muslims, is very large and has 12 mosques. The city where the king resides lies at a distance of 6 miles [10 km] and is called al-Ghaba, which means 'the forest.' The region between the two cities is covered with houses built of wood and stone."

El Bekri's account was based on tales he had heard from traders who had been in the region. The first city mentioned by El Bekri was the base for merchants. The second city, in addition to being the site of the royal palace, was the setting for religious rites. The two cities ultimately merged into one. Most of the houses were made of wood and clay, but some of the wealthier merchants lived in stone dwellings. At its peak, the capital had a population of 30,000 people. El Bekri described the government and religion: "The king has interpreters, a treasurer, and chooses most of his viziers [advisers] from among the Muslim population. The [non-Muslim] religion is pagan and consists of idol worship."

El Bekri also gave details of the empire's wealth: "All gold nuggets found in the mines belong to the king, but he gives the gold dust to his subjects." Of the empire's military strength, El Bekri states: "The king of Ghana can raise an army of 200,000 men, 40,000 of whom are armed with bows and arrows." Other reports indicate that the people of Ghana lived in great luxury, wearing woolen, silk, and velvet clothing. The king's palace had the finest sculpture, painting, and glasswork; his stables contained hundreds of horses, which walked on carpets and were tied with silken ropes.

The ancient adobe mosque at Djenné is widely regarded as the finest example of Sudanese mud-brick architecture in Africa.

the Senegal basin, was transported north, where it was traded for Saharan salt. Ghana also exported kola nuts, ivory, and slaves. At stations along the trade routes, it imposed taxes on salt, textiles, copperware, Egyptian horses, and tools, some of which came all the way from Europe. Ghana also established an extensive system for the collection of income tax.

Ghana reached its peak under the Soninke elite, around 1050 CE. However, the capital city was conquered and plundered in 1076 CE by the Almoravids (a militant Muslim sect of the Sanhaja Berbers in Morocco), and the empire disintegrated as the peoples of western Africa withdrew their allegiance and formed independent kingdoms. Around 1200 CE, people from Takrur, a rival state in western Africa, took control of Ghana. They were then themselves challenged by the Malinke people of Kangaba, another kingdom in the region. In 1235 CE, the Malinke king Sundiata Keita defeated the Takrur at the Battle of Kirina and razed the capital at Kumbi Saleh. Sundiata Keita then founded the kingdom of Mali, which became the main power in the region.

Mali

The founding of the kingdom of Mali by Sundiata Keita was immortalized in the oral tradition by *griots* (itinerant singer-poets) of the Malinke, a subgroup among the Mandé people of western Africa.

Sundiata Keita (Mari Jata; Mari the Great), a Muslim who had come to the throne of a small state on the upper Niger River in 1230 CE, expanded his new empire by conquering the neighboring tribal domains. He made his own birthplace, Niani (near the border of Mali and Guinea), the capital of the empire. He introduced cotton cultivation and textile manufacture, but his empire's main strength lay in trade; his traders established posts throughout western Africa, creating links to the long-distance trade routes between Asia and Africa and, via the Mediterranean, to Europe. Sundiata Keita also developed an efficient system for taxing trade.

In 1255 CE, Sundiata Keita drowned while attempting to get across the Sankarini River. He was succeeded by a line of capable Muslim Mali kings, the greatest of whom was his great-nephew Mansa Musa (ruled 1312–1337 CE), who conquered the cities of Timbuktu and Gao and expanded the Mali Empire. Mansa Musa was a devout Muslim who went on a widely celebrated hajj (pilgrimage) to Mecca, a journey he undertook at the head of a vast caravan comprising hundreds of camels and thousands of people. In July of 1324 CE, he passed through Cairo, where he distributed so many gifts of gold that he caused inflation throughout Egypt. On reaching Mecca, he met the Arabian poet and architect Es Saheli and persuaded him to travel to Mali. Es Saheli encouraged Mansa Musa to import Muslim teachers and to build schools, including a university in Timbuktu.

An eyewitness account of the Mali Empire in the mid-14th century CE was written by Ibn Battuta of Tangiers, an Arab traveler who had visited India, China, Indonesia, and Turkestan before

This wooden sculpture of a mother and child was carved in Mali in the 14th century CE.

This mud-built monument in Gao (a city in modern Mali) is believed to be the tomb of the Songhai emperor Askia Muhammad I (ruled 1493–1528 CE).

Songhai

The Songhai people originally made their capital at Gao as early as the seventh century CE. The city grew rich on trade but was conquered and incorporated into the Mali Empire by Mansa Musa in 1325 CE. However, Songhai rule was reestablished there in the 15th century CE, and under Sunni Ali (ruled 1465–1492 CE), the kingdom of the Songhai became a great empire. Ali (also known as Ali the Great) incorporated eastern Mali and the central Niger region into his empire. Supported by a powerful army and a navy on the Niger River, he captured the trading city of Djenné in 1473 CE.

Ali was succeeded in 1493 CE by one of his generals, Muhammad Touré, who ruled as Askia Muhammad I until 1528 CE. (The name Askia, meaning "the forceful one," was reputedly given to him by one of Sunni Ali's daughters.) Askia Muhammad extended his empire by conquest eastward as far as Lake Chad and westward almost to the Atlantic Ocean. Around 1500 CE, he captured Agadez (in modern Niger), an important city at the convergence of trade routes to and from Tripoli and the Nile River Valley. He seized the salt mines under the control of Agadez and had irrigation canals constructed to turn parts of the desert into arable land. Agadez was also an important post for the trade in slaves, who were sold to Arabs farther north.

In 1513 CE, Askia Mohammad extended his control of trade routes by annexing Kano (a city on the Hadejia River), which was important for the trade in leather, gold, salt, ivory, and slaves. He introduced bureaucratic government, standardized trade regulations, and oversaw the policing of the trade routes.

Askia Mohammad also promoted literacy and learning across the empire. He was a devout Muslim who, in 1496 CE, had made a hajj to Mecca, where he had

arriving in Niani in 1353 CE. By that time, Mansa Musa had been succeeded by his son, Mansa Maghan (ruled 1337–1341 CE), who had then been succeeded by Mansa Musa's brother, Mansa Süleyman (ruled 1341–1360 CE). Ibn Battuta reported: "The sultan's daily dress is a red velvet tunic. He is preceded by musicians, who carry gold and silver guitars, and followed by 300 armed slaves. When he sits down, they play trumpets, drums, and horns." He praised the locals' belief in justice and their strong sense of law and order: "Complete freedom reigns in the land. Neither travelers nor the inhabitants have reason to fear robbers or violent men."

In the mid-15th century CE, the Mali Empire was eclipsed by the Songhai Empire, which became the preeminent trading state in western Africa until around 1600 CE. A smaller Mali kingdom continued to exist.

been appointed caliph (Islamic leader) of western Sudan. Under him, Timbuktu enjoyed a great flowering of literature and Muslim scholarship and became an even greater cultural center than it had been under the Mali.

In 1528 CE, when he was more than 80 years old, Askia Mohammad was deposed by his son. Askia Mohammad is believed to be buried in a mud-built monument in Gao known as the Tomb of Askia. The monument includes two mosques, a cemetery, and an assembly ground, as well as a pyramidal tomb.

Indigenous authors rose to prominence during the time of the Songhai Empire. Ahmad Baba (1556–1627 CE) wrote works on Islamic law that have remained useful works of reference into the 21st century CE. Other scholars translated the works of ancient Greek authors, such as Plato and Aristotle, and wrote treatises on astronomy and mathematics. Lost for hundreds of years, the works were rediscovered in 1851 CE in the Baguirmi area, south of Lake Chad.

The Songhai Empire endured until 1591 CE, when it was toppled by a cavalry invasion by Moroccans in search of gold mines. Minor kingdoms such as Gonja, Ségou, and Kaarta arose, vying to fill the power vacuum left by the Songhai. None of those states achieved dominance, however.

Kanem and Bornu

The Kanem Empire was established to the northeast of Lake Chad and built its prosperity on the trans-Saharan trade route that carried ivory and slaves to the region surrounding Tripoli (in modern Libya). The first Kanem rulers were the Zaghawa (or Duguwa), the dominant

members of a confederation of nomads. They were succeeded by the Sayfuwa, who converted to Islam around the time that they took power in the 11th century CE. The Sayfuwa expanded their lands through conquest, and by the 13th century CE, the Kanem Empire extended as far as Kano (in modern Nigeria) to the west, Wadai (in modern Chad) to the east, the Fezzan region (in modern Libya) to the north, and the Adamawa grasslands (in modern Cameroon) to the south. The capital of the Kanem Empire was Njimi.

In the 14th century CE, the Bulala people (from the region of Lake Fitri in central Chad) drove the Sayfuwa rulers westward into the Bornu region (to the west of Lake Chad). Initially, the Sayfuwa lived as nomads, but around 1472 CE,

This bronze plaque depicts a warrior chief of the Bini people, whose kingdom lasted from the 12th century CE to 1897 CE.

These artifacts— two breastplates, a sankyo (a flutelike musical instrument), a bell, and a drum— were all made from pure gold by Ashanti craftsmen in the 19th century CE.

their *mai* (ruler), Ali Dunamami, established a new fortified capital at Ngazargamu (in modern Nigeria) and began to build the Bornu Empire.

Under Ali Gaji (ruled 1497–1515 CE), the Sayfuwa recaptured Njimi but continued to rule from Ngazargamu over the Kanem-Bornu Empire. Idris Alooma (ruled 1571–1603 CE) greatly increased imperial power using military camps, scorched-earth tactics, Berber camels, and musketeers armed with weapons purchased from the Ottoman Turks. Idris Alooma took control of the trade routes to Egypt. He was also a notable diplomat who established links with Egypt and Tripoli as well as with the Ottomans. After Idris Alooma's death, the power of the empire faded in the 17th century CE, but it survived in a weakened form until 1846 CE, when it was taken over by the Wadai Empire to the east.

Other western kingdoms

The Hausa peoples established several independent city-states that survived from the late 9th century CE to the late 16th century CE and peaked around 1400 CE. Lying between the Songhai on the Niger River and Kanem-Bornu in the region of Lake Chad, the Hausa city-states were Biram, Daura, Zaria, Rano, Gobir, Katsina, and Kano; the last two were major urban centers of commerce, made rich by trans-Saharan trade. In the 14th century CE, they all converted to Islam and were repeatedly subjected to conquest by the larger kingdoms of western Africa.

The Edo (or Bini) peoples founded the kingdom of Benin in the 12th century CE. From a capital at Benin City, their *obas* (kings) ruled over most of what is today southern Nigeria. Oba Ozolua (ruled c. 1480–1504 CE) established a slave trade with Portugal that continued until the 18th century CE. Benin was annexed to British Nigeria in 1897 CE.

The Ashanti peoples formed a confederation in the early 18th century CE. Their kingdom, in what is now central Ghana, reached its peak around 1750 CE. As they tried to subdue the rival Fanti peoples, the Ashanti encountered the British and fought against both until 1826 CE. The Ashanti capital, Kumasi (now in Ghana), was burned in 1873 CE during another round of fighting with the British. Prempeh I, head chief of the Ashanti from 1888 CE, was captured in 1896 CE and exiled by the British to the Seychelles (a group of islands in the Indian Ocean), but he was reinstated in 1926 CE.

The Yoruba peoples established the kingdom of Oyo in territory between the Volta and Niger rivers around 1400 CE. They created an empire that flourished around 1650 to 1750 CE, but by the early 19th century CE, it had collapsed into several small kingdoms and eventually fell under British control.

The kingdom of Dahomey was founded on the coast of the Gulf of Guinea in the early 17th century CE. It expanded from its capital, Abomey, in the 18th century CE and profited from the slave trade, notably under Agaja (ruled 1708–1732 CE), who seized the coastal town of Allada and traded directly with European slave merchants. Gézo (ruled 1818–1858 CE) added inland territory as the French arrived on the coast. The French later defeated Béhanzin (ruled 1889–1894 CE), and the kingdom became part of French West Africa. In 1960 CE, the colony gained independence as the Republic of Dahomey; in 1975 CE, it was renamed Benin.

Eastern Africa

In eastern Africa, Bantu tribes arriving around 1000 CE assimilated the indigenous San peoples. Arab traders established ports, colonized the coast, and intermarried with the Bantu population, developing a new culture and language—Swahili. They established several coastal city-states, including Mogadishu, Mombasa, Malindi, Lamu, Kilwa, Pate, and Sofala. The ruling Arab Africans grew rich exporting gold, ivory, and slaves (many of them Bantu).

Inland, peoples of unknown origin moved down the Nile River to settle in the interlake areas and establish complex societies in the 14th century CE. The Bachwezi dynasty created a kingdom between Lake Victoria and Lake Edward in the late 14th century CE. Luo people from Sudan took control of the kingdom around 1500 CE. They drove the Bachwezi south to the kingdom of Rwanda, which had been established in the 15th century CE by the indigenous

These 13th-century-CE walls at Great Zimbabwe used to surround an enclosure for the ruler's wives and mother.

Bututsi peoples. The Luo then established the kingdoms of Ankole and Buganda (parts of modern Uganda) and Karagwe (part of modern Tanzania). In Rwanda, the Bachwezi established rule over the Bututsi by the 16th century CE.

Central Africa

Having discovered major deposits of gold and grown rich through trading, the Karanga people (descendants of the Bantu) established the Mwene Mutapa Empire around 800 CE. The Karanga civilization was the earliest and most advanced in the region, and it endured for 1,000 years. At its height (c. 1450–1500 CE), it ruled over the lands between the Zambezi and Limpopo rivers (modern Zimbabwe and Mozambique).

The Karanga began building Great Zimbabwe, a city and religious center, around 1100 CE. Construction was not completed until the 15th century CE, by which time Great Zimbabwe was probably home to around 18,000 people. Today, the ruins—17 miles (28 km) southeast of Masvingo—cover 100 acres (40 ha), and most of them are still contained by a stone wall that is 30 feet (9 m) tall. The word *Zimbabwe*, which gives its name to the modern nation, probably means "stone houses."

The Mwene Mutapa Empire declined sharply in the 16th century CE before disintegrating through factional fighting. In 1629 CE, it became a vassal state of Portugal. Thereafter, survivors of the ruling dynasty established a new kingdom called Karanga in Mozambique; it survived until 1902 CE.

This 19th-century-CE wooden figure depicts a Luba girl wearing beads and with traditional stripes cut into her skin (scarification).

In western central Africa, the kingdom of Kongo was established in the 14th century CE. At the height of its power, around 1500 CE, it governed land stretching from the Atlantic Ocean as far east as the Kwango River and from the Congo River in the north as far south as the Kwana River. The kingdom fell to Portuguese slave traders in the 17th century CE.

In the heart of central Africa, to the east of Lake Tanganyika, the Luba people under chief Kongolo embarked on the creation of the Luba Empire around 1500 CE. The empire's economic strength, based on trading copper and palm oil, was at its height under a succession of strong rulers between 1780 and 1874 CE. In the late 19th century CE, the Luba Empire was conquered by Belgium. It then became part of the Congo Free State and later part of the Belgian Congo before becoming independent in 1960 CE as the Democratic Republic of Congo.

Around 1600 CE, one of the sons of the Luba chief Kongolo founded a separate dynasty and a new state, the Lunda Empire, on the southern border of his father's domains—on lands that are now part of the modern Democratic Republic of Congo, northeastern Angola, and northwestern Zambia. The Lunda Empire eventually divided into the states of the Bemba, Kasanje, and Kazembe. The largest of these states was Kazembe, which was dominant from 1750 to 1850 CE. In the late 19th century CE, the Lunda Empire was divided among three European colonial powers: the Portuguese in Angola, the Belgians in the Congo Free State, and the British in northwestern Rhodesia.

Southern Africa

After around 1000 CE, the indigenous Khoikhoi and San peoples of southern Africa were dominated by Bantu immigrants. The descendants of the eastern branch of Bantu were the Shona, Xhosa, Kikuyu, and Zulu peoples, while the descendants of the western branch were the Herero and Tonga peoples.

The Zulu leader Shaka (c. 1787–1828 CE) created an empire in southern Africa. At the start of his rule, in 1816 CE, Shaka attempted to unite the neighboring Bantu tribes in what is now the South African province of KwaZulu-Natal. When that plan failed, he took up arms against them and unleashed the *mfecane* (Zulu for "crushing"), an era of warfare during which many indigenous peoples were expelled from their lands.

The period of social dislocation and migration that followed led to the creation of several new kingdoms. Tribes left the Zulu area in all directions. Sobhuza, chief of the Ndwandwe peoples, went north and established the Swazi kingdom. Another chief, Moshesh, formed the Basotho kingdom in what is now Lesotho. Another Ndwandwe chief, Soshangane, led his fighting men into what is now Mozambique, where he defeated the Tsonga people and established an empire that he named Gaza, after his grandfather. The Gaza Empire survived until 1895 CE, when it fell to the Portuguese. The Kololo chief Sebetwane traveled north and seized the region of Barotseland (now part of western Zambia). In 1837 CE, the Ndebele chief Mzilikazi Khumalo invaded the southern part of the Mwene Mutapa Empire and established Matabeleland (now part of western and southwestern Zimbabwe).

The Zulus who remained on their own territory were later subjected to an onslaught by white traders and settlers who came from Europe to exploit the mineral wealth of southern Africa. The Zulus resisted the invaders under three consecutive kings—Dingane (ruled 1828–1840 CE), Mpande (ruled 1840–1872 CE), and Cetshwayo (ruled 1872–1879 CE)—but were ultimately defeated by the British in 1879 CE.

This illustration, from 1836 CE, eight years after Shaka's death, depicts the Zulu leader in battle dress with a shield and a spear.

See also:

Africa's Early Cultures (volume 9, page 1256) • The Edges of the Empire (volume 5, page 582)

TIME LINE

WESTERN ASIA, NORTHERN EUROPE, AND AFRICA		REST OF THE WORLD	
c. 4 million BCE	Early hominids emerge in eastern and southern Africa.		
c. 2 million BCE	*Homo habilis* and *Homo erectus* evolve.		
c. 100,000 BCE	First modern humans develop in Africa.	**c. 30,000 BCE**	Lapita culture develops in New Guinea.
c. 15,000 BCE	Bows and arrows first used in Africa.		
c. 2000 BCE	Bronze Age begins in northern Africa.		
c. 1800 BCE	Previously fertile Sahara becomes desert.		
c. 1000 BCE	Nubia gains independence from Egypt. Copper industry flourishes in southern Congo.		
c. 700 BCE	Iron Age begins in Egypt.		
c. 50 CE	**c. 50 CE** Aksum emerges in Ethiopia.		
	c. 200 CE Iron Age methods spread to eastern and central Africa.	**220 CE**	Second Han period ends in China.
	c. 300 CE Slavs start to settle in Russia.	**c. 320 CE**	Gupta dynasty begins in India.
	330 CE Byzantium renamed Constantinople.		
	381 CE Arian heresy condemned at Council of Aquileia.		

	WESTERN ASIA, NORTHERN EUROPE, AND AFRICA		REST OF THE WORLD	
	395 CE	On death of Theodosius I, Roman Empire divided into eastern and western empires.		
	c. 400 CE	Ghana develops into empire.	c. 400 CE	Hinduism develops into approximately modern form. First settlers arrive on Easter Island.
	443 CE	Constantinople threatened by Attila the Hun.		
	476 CE	Last Roman emperor, Romulus Augustulus, deposed by German invaders.	c. 500 CE	Buddhism established in China and Thailand.
c. 550 CE	c. 550 CE	Kiev emerges as leading city in Russia.	c. 550 CE	Buddhism imported to Japan from Korea.
	570 CE	Prophet Mohammed born in Mecca.		
	629 CE	Mohammed leads first pilgrimage to Mecca.	618 CE	Chinese Tang period begins after end of Sui dynasty.
			c. 675 CE	Srivijaya kingdom starts to dominate maritime trade around Malay Archipelago.
	680 CE	Battle of Karbala causes lasting rift between Shi'ite and Sunni Muslims.	710 CE	Heijo becomes Japan's first fixed capital.
	793 CE	Vikings raid monastery on Lindisfarne island off English coast.		
	800 CE	Charlemagne is crowned Holy Roman emperor.	c. 800 CE	Khmer state begins to flourish in present-day Cambodia. Maya from Guatemalan lowlands move to highlands and into Yucatán Peninsula. Chimú kingdom becomes powerful on coast of Peru.
	847 CE	End of iconoclasm.		
	860 CE	Harald Finehair inherits small kingdom; eventually becomes first sole king of Norway.		

WESTERN ASIA, NORTHERN EUROPE, AND AFRICA		REST OF THE WORLD	
865 CE	Vikings capture Eboracum (modern York), England.		
867 CE	Basil I founds Macedonian dynasty.		
c. 878 CE	Danelaw created in English midlands.		
885 CE	Viking forces lay siege to Paris.	c. 900 CE	Toltecs become major power in central and southern Mexico. Start of Postclassic period.
911 CE	Danish Viking Rollo becomes first duke of Normandy.		
982 CE	Erik the Red reaches Greenland.		
988 CE	Russia adopts Orthodox Christianity.		
c. 1000 CE			
c. 1000 CE	Mahmud begins campaigns in Persia, Afghanistan, and India that lead to creation of Ghaznavid Empire.	c. 1000 CE	Leif Eriksson lands in America. Chichén Itzá captured by Toltecs. Anasazi and Mississippian peoples emerge around this time.
1016 CE	England united with Denmark and Norway under Cnut the Great.		
1018 CE	Bulgaria becomes part of Byzantine Empire.		
1071 CE	Turks defeat Byzantine forces at Battle of Manzikert.		
1095 CE	First Crusade proclaimed by Pope Urban II.		
1099 CE	Crusaders succeed in taking Jerusalem.		

WESTERN ASIA, NORTHERN EUROPE, AND AFRICA		REST OF THE WORLD	
1145 CE	Second Crusade launched by Eugenius III.		
1147 CE	Crusader army defeated by Turks at Battle of Dorylaeum.	c. 1162 CE	Genghis Khan born.
1187 CE	Saladin captures Jerusalem. Pope Gregory VIII calls Third Crusade.		
1198 CE	Pope Innocent III initiates Fourth Crusade.	c. 1200 CE	Nomadic Mexica people settle on Lake Texcoco.
1204 CE	Constantinople sacked during Fourth Crusade.		
1215 CE	English barons force King John to allow Magna Carta.	1215 CE	Genghis Khan razes Yenking (modern Beijing).
1235 CE	Kingdom of Mali founded in western Africa.		
1240 CE	Kiev sacked by Mongol army.		
1244 CE	Turkish and Egyptian forces take Jerusalem.		
1250 CE — 1250 CE	Mamluks take power in Egypt.		
1256 CE	Il-Khanate established.		
1258 CE	Osman I, founder of Ottoman Empire, born. Mongols sack Baghdad.		
1260 CE	Mongols defeated by Mamluks at Battle of Ain Jalut.	1279 CE	Mongol leader Kublai Khan completes conquest of China.

WESTERN ASIA, NORTHERN EUROPE, AND AFRICA		REST OF THE WORLD	
1281 CE	Osman I takes control of small emirate in Anatolia, sowing seeds for Ottoman Empire.	1281 CE	Typhoon destroys Mongol force during attempted invasion of Japan.
1290 CE	Mamluk dynasty ends in Egypt.	c. 1300 CE	Anasazi and Mississippian peoples decline and disappear.
1313 CE	Khan of Golden Horde converts to Islam.	c. 1345 CE	Tenochtitlán and other Aztec cities emerge.
1360 CE	Murad I takes power; Ottoman Empire expands into Balkans and Anatolia.	1368 CE	Ming dynasty begins in China after expulsion of Mongols.
1382 CE	Moscow captured by Mongols of the Golden Horde.		
1396 CE	Bayezid I defeats Christian alliance at Battle of Nicopolis.	1398 CE	Mongols under leadership of Tamerlane attack Delhi.

c. 1400 CE

WESTERN ASIA, NORTHERN EUROPE, AND AFRICA		REST OF THE WORLD	
c. 1400 CE	Hausa and Yoruba peoples dominate along Niger River.	c. 1400 CE	Aztecs oust Tepanecs as major power in region. Main cities—Tenochtitlán, Texcoco, and Tlacopán—form triple alliance and subjugate much of Central America.
1402 CE	Tamerlane defeats Ottomans at Battle of Ankara.		
1410 CE	Lithuania defeats Teutonic Knights at Battle of Tannenberg.		
c. 1450 CE	Songhai succeeds Mali in western Africa.	c. 1450 CE	Malacca becomes first Southeast Asian state to adopt Islam.
1453 CE	Constantinople falls to Ottoman Turks.		
1485 CE	Russia ends tributes to Mongols.	c. 1458 CE	Aztecs conquer Mixtec cities.

WESTERN ASIA, NORTHERN EUROPE, AND AFRICA		REST OF THE WORLD	
1517 CE	Protestant Reformation begins.		
1520 CE	Süleyman I takes power in Ottoman Empire; arts and culture flourish during his 46-year reign.		
1521 CE	Ottoman army under Süleyman I takes city of Belgrade.	1521 CE	Aztec forces overwhelmed by Spanish; end of Aztec Empire and culture.
1522 CE	Ottomans drive Knights Hospitaller from island of Rhodes.		
1533 CE	Accession of Ivan the Terrible, first "Czar of All the Russias."	1533 CE	Spanish topple Inca Empire.
1538 CE	Ottoman fleet commanded by Khayr ad-Din defeats Christian fleet at Battle of Preveza.		
1546 CE	Protestant reformer Martin Luther dies.	1549 CE	Francis Xavier arrives in Japan.
1555 CE	Süleyman signs peace treaty with Safavids.		
1566 CE	Süleyman I dies.		
1591 CE	Songhai conquered by Moroccans.	1584 CE	English make first attempt to colonize North America.
c. 1600 CE	Dahomey founded in central Africa.	1607 CE	English establish Jamestown Colony in Virginia.
1750 CE	Ashanti dominate central Ghana.		
1879 CE	British defeat Zulus.	1769 CE	English mariner James Cook arrives in Tahiti.

c. 1600 CE

GLOSSARY

Abbasids dynasty of caliphs formed by descendants of Mohammed's uncle Abbas; ruled from Baghdad (750–1258 CE) until it was sacked by Mongols. Accorded a purely religious function in Egypt, Abbasids held power there from 1261 to 1517 CE.

Albigensians Christian heretics in southern France in the 12th and 13th centuries CE. They were attacked by the Albigensian Crusade in 1209 CE and were finally destroyed by the Inquisition.

Almohads Islamic reformers from northern Africa who drove the Almoravids out of southern Spain in 1146 CE, establishing a strong caliphate.

Almoravids fundamental Muslim tribe from the southern Sahara who conquered northern Africa and aided the Muslims in Córdoba against the Christians between 1086 and 1146 CE.

Anatolia another name for Asia Minor (part of modern Turkey).

Arianism doctrine of fourth-century-CE theologian Arius; held that Jesus Christ was not of the same substance as God, but merely the best of created beings.

Assyrians people of northern Mesopotamia whose independent state, established in the 14th century BCE, became a major power in the region.

Australopithecus "southern ape"; an upright-walking hominid from around 4 million years ago; found in Africa.

Bantu people of Africa, south of the equator, who speak related languages. After around 1000 BCE, they occupied large portions of Africa, leaving the area around Lake Chad and mixing with agricultural people.

Berbers descendants of the pre-Arab inhabitants of northern Africa.

Bosporus strait, 19 miles (30 km) long, that joins the Black Sea and the Sea of Marmara.

bronze copper-tin alloy widely used by 1700 BCE.

Bronze Age period during which bronze became the most important basic material; began around 3500 BCE in western Asia and around 1900 BCE in Europe.

Buddhism religion founded by Siddharta Gautama, called the Buddha; rejected much of Hinduism, including priestly authority, the Vedic scriptures, sacrificial practices, and the caste system. Its goal is nirvana (release from all desire and from the cycle of life, death, and rebirth). The major schools of Buddhism are Theravada and Mahayana.

Bulgaria region and nation of the Balkans that constituted the strongest empire in eastern Europe in the 9th and 10th centuries CE. Incorporated into the Byzantine Empire in 1018 CE, Bulgaria rebelled in 1185 CE, forming another empire, which collapsed in the 14th century CE.

Burgundy region of eastern France that became a powerful independent state in the 15th century CE. Its main city is Dijon.

Buyids native dynasty that ruled in western Iran and Iraq in the period between the Arab and Turkish conquests (945–1055 CE).

Byzantium ancient Greek city on the shore of the Bosporus; later known as Constantinople; modern Istanbul.

caliph from *khalifah*, Arabic for "successor"; religious and political leader of Islam; successor to Mohammed. Competing caliphs divided the Islamic states.

caliphate office and realm held by a caliph.

Cathars heretical Christian sect that flourished in western Europe in the 12th and 13th centuries CE. The Cathari believed that there are two principles, one good and one evil, and that the material world is evil.

Constantinople name for Byzantium (present-day Istanbul), which became the (Christian) residence of the emperor Constantine in 330 CE. In 395 CE, it became the capital of the eastern Roman Empire.

Danelaw Viking kingdom in north-eastern England.

Dnieper fourth longest river in Europe; flows 1,367 miles (2,200 km) from the Valdai Hills to the west of Moscow to the Black Sea.

Eboracum Roman name for their fortification in northern England; later became the Viking town of Yorvick and finally the modern city of York.

Fatimids Shi'ite dynasty of caliphs in northern Africa (909–1171 CE); descended from Mohammed's daughter Fatima; conquered Egypt and founded Cairo around 969 CE.

Fifth Crusade (1217–1221 CE) expedition that conquered Lisbon in 1217 CE and Damietta in Egypt in 1219 CE. Against the pope's wishes, the crusaders tried to conquer Egyptian territory in exchange for Jerusalem, but their attempt ended in failure.

First Crusade (1095–1099 CE) led by Godfrey of Bouillon and Raymond of Toulouse; conquered Edessa, Tripoli, Antioch, and Jerusalem, making them Christian kingdoms.

Fourth Crusade (1202–1204 CE) expedition by French knights; captured Byzantium with the aid of Venice and founded a western-style empire.

Golden Horde western part of the Mongol Empire. At its peak, it included most of European Russia.

Hagia Sophia great domed Church of the Holy Wisdom in Constantinople; designed by Anthemius of Tralles and Isidorus of Miletus; built between 532 and 537 CE under Emperor Justinian.

Hanseatic League union of free cities in northern Germany that promoted their own interests in trade; formed in the 12th century CE. The leading Hanseatic centers included Bremen, Hamburg, and Lübeck. The league later grew to include non-German cities, such as Riga, Stockholm, and Szczecin.

Hausa people of northwestern Nigeria and southern Niger.

Homo erectus hominid who walked upright and lived between 500,000 and 150,000 years ago in Africa, Asia, and Europe; first hominid species to be found outside Africa; includes Java man (*Pithecanthropus*) and Peking man; used tools, made shelters, and utilized fires.

Homo habilis hominid who walked upright and lived around 2 million years ago, at the same time as *Australopithecus*; first hominid species

to be found in association with manu-factured tools.

Huns central Asiatic people noted for horsemanship and ferocity in battle; drove the Visigoths from Ukraine (c. 370 CE); conquered eastern and central Europe in the fifth century CE; seized western Europe under Attila (c. 450 CE).

iconoclasm policy of destroying religious images (icons); introduced in the eighth century CE by the Byzantine emperor Leo III.

Il-Khanate Mongol dynasty that ruled in Persia in the 13th and 14th centuries CE.

iron metallic element (chemical symbol Fe) that can be made into tools, weapons, and ornaments. It is extracted from iron ore by heating and hammering it for long periods. Iron was being processed in Anatolia, western Asia, by 3000 BCE. Iron is easier to work with than bronze.

Iron Age period during which major tools and weapons were made of iron; followed the Bronze Age. The Hittites formed the first Iron Age culture around 1700 BCE. Between 1200 and 600 BCE, ironworking spread over Asia and Europe.

Islam monotheistic religion worship-ping Allah; founded by Mohammed in the seventh century CE. Its tenets are recorded in the Koran.

Jagiellon dynasty rulers of Poland-Lithuania, Bohemia, and Hungary who wielded great power and influence in east-central Europe in the 15th and 16th centuries CE.

Janissaries army of slaves and Christian prisoners of war who were indoctrinated with Turkish culture and military discipline. They stood as the basis for the military successes the Turks enjoyed between 1360

and 1826 CE. Regular outbreaks of Janissary revolts took place from the 17th century CE onward. Their power ended in 1826 CE, when Sultan Mahmud II had them massacred.

Kiev capital of the Russian Empire of Vladimir and Yaroslav; flourishing trade center and seat of the Byzantine Church; destroyed by the Mongols in 1240 CE.

Knights Hospitaller society of Christian knights who fought the Muslims. The order grew out of the 11th-century-CE pilgrims' hospital in the Holy Land. When noblemen of the brotherhood became the leaders, the order took on a military character.

Knights Templar religious military order established at the time of the crusades to protect Christian pilgrims to the Holy Land. The order was destroyed in 1307 CE.

Mamluks originally slaves hired as mercenaries by caliphs in Cairo to maintain order in the 12th century CE; gained power in 1250 CE; dominated Egypt until the start of the 16th century CE.

Mongols Asian tribes of horsemen who originally came from lands to the north of China; united by Genghis Khan in 1190 CE; conquered central Asian Islamic states, China, Russia, and the Delhi Sultanate in the 12th and 13th centuries CE.

Moscow city that became the seat of Byzantine Russian Christianity after the fall of Kiev. Moscow separated from the Mongols in the 14th century CE and assumed the leadership of all the Russian principalities. After the conquest of Byzantium, Moscow became the new Christian center.

Mughals Muslim dynasty that ruled India (1526–1857 CE); founded by Babur, a descendant of Genghis Khan.

Muslims worshippers of Allah; members of Islam.

Nika Revolt uprising (January 13–18, 532 CE) in Constantinople of the Greens and the Blues, who turned the population against Justinian. The population appointed a new emperor and destroyed the city center. Belisarius suppressed the revolt with mercenaries.

Nile world's longest river at 4,132 miles (6,650 km). The river flows north from central Africa into Egypt, where in the final part of its course it forms a delta before reaching the Mediterranean Sea. During the annual rainy season in central Africa, the Nile River floods its banks, rendering the surrounding valley fertile and suitable for agriculture and horticulture.

Novgorod Russian trading post and manufacturing center for the German *hansas*, which monopolized trade in the North Sea and the Baltic Sea. Novgorod came under Mongol threat in the 13th century CE. Ivan III conquered the city in 1478 CE.

Ostrogoths Germanic tribe from Ukraine; subjected by the Huns; migrated to Hungary in the fifth century CE; established a kingdom in Italy under Theodoric (493 CE); defeated under Totila (552 CE).

Pechenegs seminomadic Turkic people who occupied the steppes to the north of the Black Sea; became a threat to Byzantium in the 10th century CE.

Phoenicia country north of Israel and Palestinian areas (modern Lebanon) consisting of mountains and a narrow coastal strip. It was inhabited by local groups, mainly Canaanites. After Egyptian rule (c. 1500–1350 BCE) and Hittite rule (c. 1350–1200 BCE), Phoenicia became independent around 1100

BCE. Phoenician forests were used for shipbuilding and timber export.

Prester John mythical Christian ruler of an unspecified land in the East. Western nations hoped that he would join forces with them against the Mongols and the Muslims.

Second Crusade (1145–1148 CE) authorized by the pope after the Turks had conquered Edessa and threatened Jerusalem. The Christians unsuccessfully besieged Damascus and returned home empty-handed.

Seljuks Turks who named themselves after their deceased leader; captured Baghdad from the Shi'ites; established power in Persia around 1055 CE; conquered Anatolia in 1071 CE. Their kingdom disintegrated by the end of the 12th century CE.

Shi'ites supporters of Mohammed's son-in-law Ali; seceded from orthodox Islam after the murder of Hussein in 680 CE. Shi'ites (from *shi'ah*, Arabic for "partisan") believe that their leaders (imams) are divinely guided and have the right to Muslim leadership.

Songhai state in western Africa (present-day Mali, Niger, and Nigeria) that flourished as a trading nation in the 15th and 16th centuries CE.

Teutonic Knights order of knights in northern Germany and the Baltic states. Founded in 1198 CE, they were defeated at the Battle of Tannenberg in 1410 CE. By the end of the 15th century CE, they had lost their political influence.

Third Crusade (1187–1192 CE) followed the capture of Jerusalem in 1187 CE. Frederick I Barbarossa, Philip II Augustus, and Richard the Lionheart traveled to Palestine. Christians conquered the fortress of Acre, but Jerusalem remained in Turkish hands.

Visigoths Germanic people from Ukraine; driven out by the Huns; settled south of the Danube River as *foederati* (allies) of Rome; rebelled in 378 CE; plundered Rome under Alaric in 410 CE; established a kingdom in Spain conquered by the Arabs in 711 CE.

Volga longest river in Europe; flows 2,193 miles (3,530 km) from northwest of Moscow to the Caspian Sea.

Volhynia area of northwestern Ukraine that was a principality from the 10th century to the 14th century CE and then became part of Lithuania.

MAJOR HISTORICAL FIGURES

Aethelred the Unready king of the English between 978 and 1016 CE; failed to prevent the Danish conquest of the country.

Alexius I Comnenus Byzantine emperor between 1081 and 1118 CE; partially restored the strength of the empire after its defeats by the Normans and the Turks in the 11th century CE.

Alfred the Great king of Wessex, a Saxon kingdom in southwestern England, between 871 and 899 CE; prevented England from falling to the Danes.

Alp Arslan Seljuk sultan who ruled between 1063 and 1072 CE; conquered Georgia, Armenia, and much of Asia Minor.

Attila king of the Huns between 434 and 453 CE; conquered western Europe; defeated in Gaul by Romans and Visigoths in 451 CE; plundered Italy in 452 CE.

Charlemagne Frankish king from 768 to 814 CE; founded the Holy Roman Empire, of which he was emperor from 800 CE.

Cnut (died 1035 CE) Danish king who united Denmark, England, and Norway into a single kingdom; also known as Canute.

Constantine the Great Roman emperor between 306 and 337 CE; ruled initially in the west only but became absolute sovereign in 324 CE; built Constantinople; legalized Christianity.

Eriksson, Leif (c. 970–1020 CE) Norse explorer; first European to reach the shores of North America.

Frederick I Barbarossa Holy Roman emperor between 1152 and 1190 CE; as a scion of the Hohenstaufen family, made peace with the Guelph leader, Henry of Saxony; strengthened his power and removed many privileges from the princes and dukes of his realm; fought against the rebellious Lombard League, the Guelphs, and the pope; died during the Third Crusade.

Genghis Khan (c. 1162–1227 CE) first leader to unite the Mongols, whom he led on a campaign of conquest that took in China and some Islamic empires.

Harald Finehair first king of a united Norway; ruled between 860 and 930 CE.

Honorius western Roman emperor between 395 and 423 CE; ruled from the age of 12.

Hulagu Khan grandson of Genghis Khan; founded the Il-Khanate dynasty in 1256 CE; seized and sacked Baghdad.

Ivan IV (the Terrible) first "Czar of All the Russias"; ruled between 1533 and 1584 CE; introduced an effective central administration and created an empire that incorporated non-Slav states.

John I Tzimisces Byzantine emperor; ruled between 969 and 976 CE; consolidated power in the Balkans and Syria.

Kublai Khan Mongolian general and statesman; grandson of Genghis Khan; ruled between 1260 and 1294 CE. He conquered China and became the first emperor of its Yüan, or Mongol, dynasty. In that role, he promoted the integration of Chinese and Mongol civilizations.

Leo III Byzantine emperor between 717 and 741 CE; sometimes known as Leo the Isaurian; gained the throne after several succession conflicts; withstood an Arab siege; made the Byzantine Empire a buffer against Islamic expansion.

Philip II Augustus king of France; ruled between 1180 and 1223 CE; annexed French territories that had previously been apportioned to the English king; expanded his powers by instituting a nonfeudal government system; forged the French kingdom into a powerful unity.

Raymond of Toulouse (1042–1105 CE) southern French nobleman; one of the leaders of the First Crusade.

Richard I (the Lionheart) king of England; ruled between 1189 and 1199 CE; took part in the Third Crusade; warred against Philip II Augustus of France.

Robert Guiscard (c. 1015–1085 CE) Norman adventurer who became duke of Apulia and extended Norman rule over Naples, Calabria, and Sicily; laid the foundations of the kingdom of Sicily.

Süleyman I sultan of the Ottoman Empire; ruled between 1520 and 1566 CE; conquered Rhodes and Belgrade; reorganized the state and tolerated different religions.

Tamerlane (Timur the Lame) Mongolian ruler between around 1369 and 1405 CE; subjected the Mongols in the west; conquered territory in Persia, India, Syria; spread Islam.

RESOURCES FOR FURTHER STUDY

BOOKS

Berinstain, Valerie. *India and the Mughal Dynasty*. New York, 1998.

Besançon, Alain (translated by Jane Marie Todd). *The Forbidden Image: An Intellectual History of Iconoclasm*. Chicago, IL, 2000.

Boulton, D'Arcy Jonathan Dacre, and Jan R. Veenstra (eds.). *The Ideology of Burgundy: The Promotion of National Consciousness, 1364–1565*. Boston, MA, 2006.

Bradbury, Jim. *Philip Augustus: King of France, 1180–1223*. New York, 1998.

Brett, Michael. *The Berbers*. Cambridge, MA, 1996.

Burns, Thomas S. *A History of the Ostro-Goths*. Bloomington, IN, 1984.

Carson, Thomas (trans. and ed.). *Barbarossa in Italy*. New York, 1994.

Collins, Roger. *Visigothic Spain, 409–711*. Malden, MA, 2004.

Comnena, Anna (translated by E.R.A. Sewter). *The Alexiad*. New York, 2003.

El-Hibri, Tayeb. *Reinterpreting Islamic Historiography: Harun al-Rashid and the Narrative of the Abbasid Caliphate*. New York, 1999.

Eraly, Abraham. *The Mughal Throne: The Saga of India's Great Emperors*. London, England, 2003.

Halperin, Charles J. *Russia and the Golden Horde: The Mongol Impact on Medieval Russian History*. Bloomington, IN, 1985.

Hartog, Leo de. *Genghis Khan: Conqueror of the World*. New York, 2004.

Haywood, John. *The Penguin Historical Atlas of the Vikings*. New York, 1995.

Heather, Peter (ed.). *The Visigoths from the Migration Period to the Seventh Century: An Ethnographic Perspective*. Rochester, NY, 1999.

Iggulden, Conn. *Genghis: Birth of an Empire*. New York, 2007.

Kennedy, Hugh. *Mongols, Huns, and Vikings: Nomads at War*. London, England, 2002.

Kimmel, Elizabeth Cody. *Before Columbus: The Leif Eriksson Expedition*. New York, 2003.

Klingel, Cynthia Fitterer, and Robert B. Noyed. *Leif Eriksson: Norwegian Explorer*. Chanhassen, MI, 2003.

Lansing, Carol. *Power and Purity: Cathar Heresy in Medieval Italy*. New York, 1998.

Le Tourneau, Roger. *The Almohad Movement in North Africa in the Twelfth and Thirteenth Centuries*. Princeton, NJ, 1969.

Madariaga, Isabel de. *Ivan the Terrible: First Tsar of Russia*. New Haven, CT, 2005.

Mainstone, R.J. *Hagia Sophia: Architecture, Structure, and Liturgy of Justinian's Great Church*. New York, 1988.

———. *Kublai Khan: From Xanadu to Superpower*. London, England, 2006.

Marozzi, Justin. *Tamerlane: Sword of Islam, Conqueror of the World*. London, England, 2004.

Martin, Janet. *Medieval Russia: 980–1584*. New York, 2007.

Miller, David. *Richard the Lionheart: The Mighty Crusader*. New York, 2003.

Nicholson, Helen J. *The Knights Hospitaller*. Rochester, NY, 2003.

Nicolle, David. *Teutonic Knight, 1190–1561*. New York, 2007.

———. *The Mongol Warlords: Genghis Khan, Kublai Khan, Hulegu, Tamerlane*. New York, 1990.

Norwich, John Julius. *A Short History of Byzantium*. New York, 1997.

Paine, Sheila. *The Golden Horde: Travels from the Himalaya to Karpathos*. New York, 1997.

Payne, Robert, and Nikita Romanoff. *Ivan the Terrible*. New York, 1975.

Pegg, Mark Gregory. *A Most Holy War: The Albigensian Crusade and the Battle for Christendom*. New York, 2008.

Quigley, Mary. *Ancient West African Kingdoms: Ghana, Mali, and Songhai*. Chicago, IL, 2002.

Ralls, Karen. *Knights Templar Encyclopedia: The Essential Guide to the People, Places, Events, and Symbols of the Order of the Temple*. Franklin Lakes, NJ, 2007.

Rawlinson, George. *Phoenicia: History of a Civilization*. New York, 2005.

Roesdahl, Else (translated by Susan M. Margeson and Kirsten Williams). *The Vikings*. New York, 1998.

Rossabi, Morris. *Khubilai Khan: His Life and Times*. Berkeley, CA, 1988.

Silverberg, Robert. *The Realm of Prester John*. Athens, OH, 1996.

Skrine, Francis Henry, and Edward Denison Ross. *The Heart of Asia: A History of Russian Turkestan and the Central Asian Khanates from the Earliest Times*. London, England, 1899.

Strayer, Joseph Reese. *The Albigensian Crusades*. Ann Arbor, MI, 1992.

Thompson, E.A. *The Huns*. Cambridge, MA, 1996.

Tracy, James D. (ed.). *The Rise of Merchant Empires: Long-Distance Trade in the Early Modern World, 1350–1750*. New York, 1990.

Turner, Ralph V., and Richard R. Heiser. *The Reign of Richard Lionheart: Ruler of the Angevin Empire, 1189–99*. New York, 2000.

Urban, William L. *The Teutonic Knights: A Military History*. St. Paul, MN, 2005.

Walker, Paul E. *Exploring an Islamic Empire: Fatimid History and Its Sources*. London, England, 2002.

Weatherford, Jack. *Genghis Khan and the Making of the Modern World*. New York, 2004.

Wiles, Maurice F. *Archetypal Heresy: Arianism Through the Centuries*. New York, 1996.

Williams, Rowan. *Arius: Heresy and Tradition*. Grand Rapids, MI, 2002.

Wilson, Derek A. *Charlemagne: A Biography*. New York, 2006.

Zamoyski, Adam. *The Polish Way: A Thousand-year History of the Poles and Their Culture*. New York, 1988.

WEB SITES

Alexiad
Web site that provides a complete text of the historical work by Anna Comnena
http://www.crusades-encyclopedia.com/alexiad.html

Berbers
Web site that gives a short and accessible introduction to the history and significance of the people who lived in northern Africa before the arrival of the Muslims
http://i-cias.com/e.o/berbers.htm

Cathars
Colorful introduction to the beliefs of the heretical group; includes links to further articles on the Albigensian Crusade and a detailed bibliography
http://www.languedoc-france.info/12_cathars.htm

Crusades
Collection of essays on the crusades; includes links to contemporary accounts and information about the various military orders
http://www.fordham.edu/halsall/sbook1k.html#General

Eriksson, Leif
Web site that outlines the explorer's career
http://www.bbc.co.uk/history/historic_figures/erikson_leif.shtml

Frederick Barbarossa
Essay on the life of the Holy Roman emperor
http://www.authorama.com/famous-men-of-the-middle-ages-22.html

Genghis Khan
Web site that describes the journey of the Mongol leader from his native land to the gates of Vienna.
http://www.fsmitha.com/h3/h11mon.htm

Golden Horde
Web site that provides an introduction to the Mongol Empire
http://www.ucalgary.ca/applied_history/tutor/islam/mongols/goldenHorde.html

RESOURCES FOR FURTHER STUDY

Hagia Sophia
Photographs and description of the so-called "mother church" of all eastern Christians
http://www.byzantines.net/epiphany/hagiasophia.htm

Iconoclasm
Essay on icons and iconoclasm in Byzantium; includes links to numerous topics of related interest
http://www.metmuseum.org/toah/hd/icon/hd_icon.htm

Ivan the Terrible
Web site that provides an introduction to the reign of the great Russian czar
http://www.mnsu.edu/emuseum/history/russia/ivantheterrible.html

Knights Hospitaller
Information about the religious military order that played a key role in the crusades
http://www.middle-ages.org.uk/knights-hospitaller.htm

Mongols
User-friendly overview of the Mongols—their culture, their conquests, and their khans
http://afe.easia.columbia.edu/mongols

Mongols and Moscow
Account of the Mongols' attacks on Russia in the 13th century CE and the subsequent rise of Muscovy
http://www.geographia.com/russia/rushis03.htm

Mughals
Web site that gives an account of the origins of the Mughals; includes references and suggestions for further study
http://www.wsu.edu/~dee/MUGHAL/CONTENTS.HTM

Ottomans
Web site that details the history of the Ottomans from their rise in the 13th century CE to their ultimate downfall almost 700 years later
http://www.wsu.edu/~dee/OTTOMAN/OTTOMAN1.HTM

Prester John
Web site that provides an overview of the numerous tales about the mythical Christian ruler
http://faculty.biu.ac.il/~barilm/presjohn.html

Richard I (the Lionheart)
Web site that gives a detailed account of the life and escapades of the Plantagenet crusader
http://www.bbc.co.uk/history/historic_figures/richard_i_king.shtml

Teutonic Knights
Web site that traces the history of the military religious order
http://www.the-orb.net/encyclop/religion/monastic/opsahl2.html

Vikings
Web site that contains information about every aspect of Viking life
http://www.bbc.co.uk/history/ancient/vikings

Visigoths
Web site that provides an account of the Visigoths' contribution to history and their relationships with other peoples of Europe
http://www.friesian.com/germania.htm

INDEX